Plays by Women: Volume Ten

The Woman Destroyed by Simone de Beauvoir, **What Happened After Nora Left Her Husband** by Elfriede Jelinek, **The Choice** by Claire Luckham and **Weldon Rising** by Phyllis Nagy

Volume Ten in Methuen's highly successful series of anthologies provides the second selection of international plays by theatre director Annie Castledine. It encompasses Diana Quick's adaptation of Simone de Beauvoir's *The Woman Destroyed* ('a more perceptive look at female loneliness I have yet to see' – *Guardian*); Tinch Minter's version of *What Happened After Nora Left Her Husband* by Elfriede Jelinek ('the most talked about and successful woman author in the German-speaking world' – Michael Hofmann, *Observer*); Claire Luckham's *The Choice* ('a rich, challenging and extraordinary drama' – *Observer*); and *Weldon Rising* by Phyllis Nagy (a 'stunning debut, a bitterly funny and chillingly surreal look at the soulless poverty of urban life . . . It's daring stuff, written with an understanding for the subtle power and violence of language' – *Independent*).

The Choice was the winner of the Martini Regional Theatre Award for Best New Play of 1992.

Annie Castledine was born in 1939 and brought up in Sheffield, South Yorkshire. The major influences in her life have been her parents, who encouraged an absolute commitment to theatre and to reading the classics before she was fifteen; Honor Matthews, Head of Drama at Goldsmiths' College, University of London (1961) who refined and extended her raw knowledge and enthusiasm; theatre directors Michael Winter, Ronald Eyre and Trevor Nunn; the work of Peter Stein and Ariane Mnouchkine and friends like Glenys Schindler, who is still introducing her to the work of women playwrights in Europe.

CITY OF BRISTOL COLLEGE

Plays by Women: Volume Ten

The Woman Destroyed
Simone de Beauvoir
adapted by Diana Quick

What Happened After Nora Left Her Husband
Elfriede Jelinek
English version by Tinch Minter

The Choice
Claire Luckham

Weldon Rising
Phyllis Nagy

Edited and Introduced by Annie Castledine

Methuen Drama

CITY OF BRISTOL
COLLEGE
00167412
822.914
04/08/10
PLA
£14.99
9780413680006
COL
WITHDRAWN

METHUEN DRAMA NEW THEATRESCRIPTS

This collection first published in Great Britain in 1994
by Methuen Drama

The Woman Destroyed adaptation and afterward copyright
© 1994 by Diana Quick
What Happened After Nora Left Her Husband version and afterward
copyright © 1994 by Tinch Minter
The Choice and afterward copyright © 1994 by Claire Luckham
Weldon Rising first published in *Plays International*, October 1992.
Copyright © 1992 by Phyllis Nagy
Selection and introduction copyright © 1994 by Annie Castledine

The authors have asserted their moral rights.

ISBN 0 413 68000 2

A CIP catalogue record for this book is available at the British Library.

Front cover photograph of Diana Quick in *The Woman Destroyed* by Christine Allsopp

Typeset by Hewer Text Composition Services, Edinburgh
Transferred to digital printing 2002

Caution
All rights whatsoever in these plays are strictly reserved. Applications for performance, broadcasting, recitation, etc, should be made before rehearsals begin to:
The Woman Destroyed and *What Happened After Nora Left Her Husband*:
Rosica Colin Limited, 1 Clareville Grove Mews, London SW7 5AH.
The Choice: Alan Brodie Representation Ltd, 211 Piccadilly, London W1J 9HF.
Weldon Rising: Casarotto Ramsay Limited, National House, 60-66 Wardour Street, London W1V 4ND.

This paperback is sold subject to the condition that it shall not, by way of trade or otherwise, be lent, resold, hired out or otherwise circulated without the publisher's prior consent in any form of binding or cover other than that in which it is published and without a similar condition, including this condition, being imposed on the subsequent purchaser.

Contents

This volume is for my niece
Helen Lakka
whom I love and honour

Introduction

Over a year ago the Artistic Director of Theatr Clwyd asked me to choose two plays to direct there in the autumn of 1993. This was both an irresistible invitation and an anxious moment of choice.

Two plays!

I want to direct so many.

Never mind all the male playwrights I may want to work with, there are so many powerful but neglected works by my own sex. I am driven by this knowledge to choose two plays by women.

My first choice, *India Song* by Marguerite Duras, is a classic example of the shameful and ignominious disregard that women writers experience throughout the whole of Europe. Marguerite Duras herself wrote about this in 1987 in her essay called 'The Theatre':

> No play by a woman had been performed at the Comédie Française since 1900, nor at Vilar's TNP, nor at the Odéon, nor at Villeurbanne, nor at the Schaubuhne, nor at Strehler's Piccolo Teatro. Not one woman playwright or one woman director . . . And then one day I got a letter from Jean-Louis Barrault asking if I'd adapt my long short story, 'Days In The Trees', for the stage. I agreed. The adaptation was rejected by the censors. The play wasn't performed until 1965. It was a great success. But none of the critics pointed out that it was the first play by a woman to be performed in France for nearly a century.

India Song had in fact been commissioned by Peter Hall for the National Theatre in 1973. It had lain around unperformed for twenty years. I have never been able to understand why the resources of this great institution had not been lavished on this anarchic, political and extraordinary text. So the production at Theatr Clwyd, co-directed by Annabel Arden and myself, was the first production of this play ever. It was a great success.

Some women are also great playwrights, but the theatre space is never shared with them. Never shared equally. Never.

The National Theatre rightly presents the wonderful David Hare trilogy this autumn but not also the Gerlind Reinshagen trilogy. Who is Gerlind Reinshagen? What is her trilogy? Gerlind Reinshagen was born in 1926 in Eastern Germany and now lives in Berlin. She is probably the greatest German writer of her age. Her trilogy of plays, *Sonntagskinder* (1976), *Das Frühlingsfest* (1980), and *Tanz, Marie!* (1987), also explores the loss of hope and looks at the hardening of reality in a Europe recovering from two world wars. It seems to me that we in this country are wilfully ignorant about the work of women playwrights in Europe. That is why I included two plays by Marieluise Fleisser in Volume Nine of *Plays By Women* and why I include Elfriede Jelinek's *What Happened After Nora Left Her Husband* in this volume. It too has never been performed in this country. I dream that one day I, or another, will be allowed to direct Ibsen's *A Doll's House* and the Jelinek in repertoire.

For my second play I chose *The Choice* by Claire Luckham. I chose this because there is another principle at stake here. That is, the second production of new plays. I had already directed *The Choice* two years ago. It was a critical and commercial success. It won the TMA Martini Award for the best new play of 1992. But it didn't travel. I chose to direct it again to see if it will. I include it in this volume because I think it is a fine piece of writing which deserves some recognition. *The Woman Destroyed* by Simone de Beauvoir, adapted by Diana Quick, and *Weldon Rising* by Phyllis Nagy did receive unanimous praise when they were performed in London and it is a great pleasure to publish them now so that they may, I hope, be performed again and again, in theatres all over this country.

It is most important that directors, Artistic Directors in particular, have access to the best work by women so there is no excuse for continuing to ignore their voices. I see it as a primary social and cultural responsibility for all those involved in theatre management to represent the perceptions and visions of our women poets in their theatre repertoire; and by represent I mean not the token inclusion of one play by a woman in the season, but a full representation of maybe eight plays out of eight by women. There are now enough important and excellently written plays by women for this to be possible and it is important to continue publishing these volumes of plays so that the texts are easily available. These volumes should be compulsory reading, excitedly seized upon by all those in control of our theatres and by all those running departments of theatre in our educational institutions. It is imperative that these collections of plays by women are not marginalised or dismissed as merely recherché. I say this because I want to honour the work of the previous two editors, Michelene Wandor and Mary Remnant, and because this is Volume Ten, a landmark and a celebration.

But there are so many more fine plays by women waiting to be performed and published. Until it is no longer an event for a play by a woman to be presented, the mission must continue.

Annie Castledine, October 1993

The Woman Destroyed

A Monologue

Simone de Beauvoir
translated and adapted by Diana Quick

She gets her revenge by talking to herself. (Flaubert)

The Woman Destroyed received its British première at the Theatre Royal, Bath, on 1 October 1991 and subsequently played at the Lyric Studio, Hammersmith.

Murielle Diana Quick

Directed by Vanessa Fielding
Designed by Michael Vale
Music by Brian Connor
Costume by Sheelagh Killeen

New Year's Eve 1967.

The drawing room of **Murielle**'*s flat.*

A window above the street: a sofa, a side-table with a packet of suppositories, some incense and matches and a tray of beauty products, including cleanser, peel-off face-mask, slices of cucumber, a knife, hand-cream, moisturiser and a hand mirror. As far away from the sofa as possible there is a telephone, completely swaddled in cotton wool.

Outside, sound of the late evening rush: car engines revving, brakes squeal, a car horn.

Section I: I Need to be Ready for Tomorrow

Murielle The tits.

She closes the curtains.

Now the stupid fairy lights on the Christmas trees can't get in but the din comes right through the walls.

Horns blaring: a traffic jam building up outside.

They're all at it. They think they're such big shots behind the wheel of the family car phoney sports job pathetic little Renault white convertible.

A white cabriolet with black upholstery that was terrific and all the boys whistled when I went by, sunglasses perched on my nose, a Hermes scarf on my head. How dare they try and serenade me in those filthy old bangers! If they'd just ram into each other right under my window, well, I'd be over the moon. The sods are shattering my eardrums and there's no more cotton wool; I used the last lot to muffle the phone, it's completely pointless but I'd rather have my ears wrecked than hear how the phone never rings.

If only I could stop this din this silence and sleep. Yesterday I couldn't I got the horrors because it was the day before today. I've taken so many sleeping pills they don't work any more and this doctor's a sadist he gave me suppositories, I can't stuff them up me like loading a gun.

I've got to get some rest it's essential. I want to give myself a chance with Tristan tomorrow; no tears no shouting. 'This situation is just not normal. Financially it's a mess. A baby needs its mother.'

I'm going to have another sleepless night I'll be at the end of my tether I'll blow it. Sods. They're running around in my head I can see them, I can hear them gorging themselves on bad foie gras and burnt turkey slobbering over it Albert and Mme Nanard, Etiennette and their brats, my mother. It's against nature for my own mother my own brother to prefer my ex to me. I don't give a shit if only they'd let me sleep, you get so you're only fit for the madhouse you'll confess anything true or false, they'd better not count on that, I'm too strong for them.

Their parties really piss me off it's grim enough on the other days. I've always loathed Christmas, and Easter, and the 14th July. Nanard perched on Papa's shoulders to see the fireworks and me, the big sister, feet on the ground squashed between their bodies just at the height of their crotches, trapped in the stench of sex coming from that crowd on heat and all Mama could say was 'Look at her grizzling again.' They stuck an ice-cream in my hand that didn't help, I chucked it away, they sighed, couldn't smack me on Bastille Day. He never touched me, I was his favourite his bloody perfect little woman. But when he pegged out she didn't have to bother any more she'd clout me round the face with her rings on. I never hit Sylvie not once. But my brother Nanard was the King. She'd take him into her bed in the morning I could hear them playing with each other. Now he says you're a liar, you're vile. Obviously he won't own up they never do and they can go to hell because I do remember. She'd stroll around her boudoir half-naked in her grubby white silk robe studded with cigarette burns with him clinging to her thigh it makes you sick mothers fooling around with their little boys and I was supposed to be like that? Oh no. Nice clean children I wanted; I wasn't having Francis turn into a pouf like Nanard. Nanard with his five children he's a nancy just the same can't fool me, you'd have to really loathe women to marry that gormless lump.

Section II: I Make no Concessions

It's not going to stop. How many are there? Hundreds of thousands in the streets of Paris. And it's the same in every town all over the world. Millions and millions of them and it can only get worse, even the sky's contaminated, soon they'll be rushing about in space like they do on the motorways and you won't be able to look at the moon without thinking of all those twats gibbering away up there. I used to love the moon, it was just like me, and now they've mucked it up like they muck up everything terrible those photos of the moon landing, a dusty grey pathetic thing, for any old sod to trample on.

I've always tried to do the right thing: I've never been one to compromise. 'Don't cheat' it's been my obsession ever since I was a baby. I can see her now, this funny little thing in a ragged little dress, Mama was so bad at taking care of me, and the kind lady lisping 'And so we love our little brother do we?' And I calmly replied 'I loathe him.' The cold; Mama's eyes. It's normal to be jealous all the books say so; what's astonishing, the thing that pleases me most is that I owned up. No concessions.

Footsteps stampeding upstairs; doorbell; greetings; 12 midnight striking; cheers.

Here's one of their farces now: Happy New Year. What's all the fuss about, just because on such and such a day at such and such a time we start a new calendar. Bored me stiff all my life, that kind of hysteria. I ought to write it down, my life. Lots of women do and they get published, waltz about, get people talking and my book would be far more interesting than their twaddle. I've been through the mill, but at least I've survived without lying and cheating and that's what will drive them mad. They'll see my name under the photo in the shop windows and the world will learn the true facts. I'll have heaps of men at my feet they're such creeps they hurl themselves at the ugliest cow if she's famous. Maybe I'd meet someone who'd know how to love me.

My father loved me. No one else.

Dance music and feet on the ceiling.

It had to happen. They are dancing about on my head. There you are that's my night wrecked. I'll be shattered tomorrow I'll have to get doped up to see Tristan and it will be a disaster. Sods. Sleep is the only good thing about being alive. Rotten sods, they're making the most of it. 'The pain in the arse downstairs can't complain, it's New Year's Eve'. Go on, have a good time, I'll get even. This pain in the arse is going to get right up your arse. I've never let anybody walk over me.

Albert was livid. 'No need to make a scene.' Oh yes indeed there was. He was dancing with Nina crotch to crotch she was sticking out her vast boobs ponging of scent but you got a whiff of the bidet under it and him jigging about with an erection like a bull. Oh yes I've made a few scenes in my time. I am still the little woman who said 'I loathe him'. Outspoken, fearless and honest.

Energetic dancing thumping on the ceiling.

They are going to come through the ceiling and collapse on my head. I can see it all it's too disgusting they are rubbing up against each other, cock against cunt it's making them wet, all those 'nice' ladies, swooning with delight because the fellow's got his end up. And every one of them is going to betray their best friend, they'll do it tonight, in the bathroom, not even lying down, dress hitched up on a sweaty arse and when you go for a pee you can't help squelching through sperm like that night I was so upset at Rose's.

Section III: I've Got to Get Back to a Normal Life

Shit I'm gasping for a drink I'm starving but it would kill me to get out of my chair and go to the kitchen.

You freeze in this dump and then when I turn the heating up the air dries out, my mouth is all dry and my nose is burning. What a cock-up. They know how to muck up the moon but they can't heat a flat. If they were smart they'd invent a robot who would fetch me a juice whenever I wanted, and take care of the housework without me having to be nice and listen to them droning on.

Mariette won't be coming tomorrow, all well and good I'm bored stiff with her old dad and his cancer. Anyway I've got her broken in, she knows her place more or less. Some of them slap rubber gloves on to do the washing up and act like the lady of the house; I wouldn't put up with that. On the other hand you don't want sluts who leave hairs in the salad and fingermarks on the doors. Tristan's a prat. I was very good with the help. I just wish they'd get on with it without all the drama. You have to train them properly just as you have to train children to turn them into proper people.

Tristan hasn't trained Francis, rotten old Mariette's left me in the lurch, the room will be a pigsty after they've been. They'll arrive with a fancy present, kisses all round I'll serve little cakes and Francis will trot out the answers his father's drummed into him, he already lies like a grown-up. I must talk to Tristan about him; it's always bad when a child's deprived of his mother, he turns into a hooligan or a nancy, you don't want that. Why am I being so bloody reasonable when my heart is breaking? All I want to do is yell, 'It's UNNATURAL to take a son away from his mother'.

'Threaten him with divorce' Dédé said. He just laughed. Men gang up on you and the law's so unfair and Tristan's got so much clout that I'll get all the blame. He'd get custody not a penny more for me and I'd lose the flat, as well. It's blackmail and I can't do a thing about it. An allowance and the flat in exchange for Francis. I am at his mercy. You can't defend yourself with no money you are less than nothing, double zero. What a clot I've been, I let all that money slip through my fingers, unselfish twit. I should have made the suckers dig deep in their pockets. If I had stayed with Florent I'd have got myself a lovely little nest-egg. But Tristan was mad about me, I took pity on him, and look what happened. The dope walked out on me just because I wouldn't grovel at his feet and treat him like some kind of Napoleon.

I'll show him. Tell him I'm going to tell the little one the truth; 'I'm not sick, I'm not sick. I only live alone because your swine of a father let me down; he sweet-talked me then he tortured me and then he practically beat me up'. Have hysterics in front of the little one, cut my wrists on their doorstep, something like that. I've got plenty of ammunition I'll use it then he'll come back to me, I won't have to be alone in this dump with those people upstairs trampling all over me and the radio next door getting me up every morning and no one to bring me a snack when I'm hungry. I can't bear it. Two weeks now the plumber has been fobbing me off when it's a woman alone they tell themselves anything will do men are such a let down when you're down they walk all over you. I show my teeth I hold my head up but they spit on a woman alone.

The porter's got a dirty laugh 'playing the radio at 10 in the morning is within the statutory regulations' as if he really thought he could put me down with fancy words. But I got my own back, four nights running on the phone, they knew it was me but they couldn't prove it. I laughed and laughed.

A man under my roof. The plumber will come, the porter will greet me politely, the neighbours will put a sock in it. Fuck it. I want some dignity I want my husband my son my own front door just like everyone else.

Section IV: I had to be a Good Mother

It will be nice to take a little eleven-year-old boy to the circus, or the zoo. I'll soon sort him out. He was less trouble than Sylvie, she was a handful, soft and sly like that shrimp Albert. I don't blame her, poor little sweetheart, they all set her against me and she was at the age when a girl loathes her mother they call it ambivalence but it's more like hate. And that's another thing they can't take. Etiennette sweated when I told her, check in Claudie's diary: furious. She'd rather not have looked, like those women who won't see a doctor in case they have got cancer that way you can still see yourself as the nice kind mama of a dear little girl. Sylvie wasn't nice I had my eyes opened when I read her diary: I face things head on. I wasn't too bothered. I know that you just have to wait; one day she'd understand and thank me for it, and tell them to fuck off. I am patient, never raised a hand to her. I was ready for it, of course, I told her 'You won't grind me down.' Stubborn as a mule, whingeing on for hours and days over nothing at all; there wasn't the slightest reason for her to see Tristan again. A girl needs a father, I learnt that the hard way but whoever said she needs two?

Albert had already made life hard enough he took everything he legally could and more I had to fight him every inch of the way he would have spoiled her rotten if I hadn't stood up to him. The frocks he wanted her to have were outrageous I didn't want my daughter turning into a tart like Mama, seventy years old skirts showing her knees paint all over her face. The other day rather than bump into her on the street I crossed over the road. I would have looked good, wouldn't I, making up with someone who looked such a fright. I bet her place is a flea-pit with all the money she wastes at the hairdresser's she could pay someone to clean up.

Section V: I'll Find a Way Out of Dying Alone

They are making me ill, my tongue is all coated and this terrifies me, these two little lumps on my thigh. I take care, I eat carefully but there is no such thing as hygiene in this world it's not just cars and factories that pollute the air it's all the millions of filthy mouths gulping it in and belching it out from morning to night; if I were to let myself think of all that bad breath swallowing me up I'd have to fly off to the desert, how do you keep yourself clean in a world gone rotten?

If I fell ill no one would lift a finger. I could even conk out with my poor over-stretched heart and no one would know a thing about it. They'd find a carcass behind the door, I'd stink, I'd have a brown puddle under me, rats snacking off my nose. No I can't bear it. I wish Tristan would come back.

Here I am withering away on the shelf; forty-three it's too young. It's not fair. I want to live it up. I was made for the good life; convertible, flat, frocks, everything.

Florent coughed up, he didn't fool around except for a bit of fun in bed he behaved like a gentleman. He wanted to sleep with me and quite right too and show me off in all the chic clubs. I was lovely, my loveliest period.

It's no good thinking of the good times no one ever takes me out any more, I sit here stewing in my own juice I'm fed up with it, fed up with it, fed up.

That pig Tristan I want him to take me out to eat or the theatre I don't put my foot down nearly enough he can just about manage to drag himself round here, either by himself or with our boy flash me a great greasy smile and then he's off within the hour. Not so much as a 'Happy New Year' tonight of all nights. Bastard! I'm bored stiff with being bored stiff it's inhuman.

Section VI: I've Got to Get Out

And they're sniggering in my head 'She's all alone' they'll laugh on the other side of their faces when Tristan comes back to me. He'll come back I'll jolly well make him. I'll go back to the dressmakers I'll give parties, cocktail parties, they'll all look at my plunging neckline in *Vogue* my breasts wouldn't shame anyone 'Have you seen Murielle's picture?' they will be well and truly fucked and Francis will tell them all about our outings. I'll spoil him rotten and their lies and slanders will stick in their throats.

Such hatred. I see too much and they don't like that they don't forgive that. Mama jealous of her daughter? Now I have seen everything. She threw me into Albert's arms to get rid of me for utterly selfish reasons, no I don't want to believe that. What a cheap trick to push me into that marriage, me, all aflame, and him, like a limp chipolata. I would have known just the kind of man for Sylvie. I was strict, oh yes, I was firm but always loving, ready for a chat, I wanted to be a friend to her. God knows I'd have kissed my mother's hands if she had been like that with me. But such a thankless child. Sylvie's dead so what? The dead aren't all saints she wouldn't budge an inch she never trusted me and there was someone special in her life a boy or maybe a girl this generation is so twisted how can you tell. But she was on red alert I couldn't find a thing even when she was dead. Appalled because I did my duty as a mother. If I'd been more selfish I'd have left her there when she ran off to her father. Without her, I could have started again; it was for her own sake that I kicked up all that fuss. Very handy for Christine and her three dopey great kids, fobbing all the donkey work off on my fifteen-year-old, poor little sausage didn't know what she was doing, getting all worked up in front of the police. Yes, that's right the police. Why muck about, the police are not just there for decoration.

Albert offering me money to give up Sylvie. Men are pathetic, money on the brain, think everything's got a price, anyway I don't give a shit about his money, fuck-all compared to what Tristan forks out. Even if I was desperate I would never sell my daughter.

'Let her go, that child gives you nothing but grief' Dédé told me. She doesn't understand what it is to be a mother she's never thought beyond her own selfish pleasure. But you can't keep taking, you have to know how to give, too.

I had so much to give Sylvie, I would have made her such a good girl and I didn't expect anything back. I was devoted to her, but she never appreciated it. It was only natural to ask her teacher's help, Sylvie said in her diary she adored her, and I assumed being a teacher she'd keep her mouth shut. Dirty-minded bookworm. There was a lot more going on between them than I ever imagined, I'm still so trusting I never think the worst; the brainy ones are all queer.

Sylvie wingeing on after that and my mother on the phone declaring I had no right to interfere with my daughter and her friends. 'Interfere' her very words. 'Well of course you never did interfere with me so don't start now, I beg you.' Quick as a flash. And I hung-up.

Sylvie would have realised in the end. That's what destroyed me at the cemetery. I told myself 'with a little more time she would have agreed with me.' It's awful to think of, blue sky, all those flowers, Albert breaking down in front of everybody dear God you have to control yourself, I did, though I knew I'd never get over it. It was me they were burying. I have been buried. They were all in league to bury me deep. Even tonight not a peep out of them. And they must know what it's like, when they're out enjoying themselves and you're alone with your grief, they must know how easy it would be to . . . They'd love it if I vanished I am a thorn in their side. Not likely! I won't give them the satisfaction. I want to live, want to live again. Tristan will come back to me, they'll give me my dues, I'll get out of this hell-hole.

Section VII: I've Got to be Heard

If I were to talk to him now I'd feel better, maybe I'd sleep then. He must be at home, he always goes to bed early he saves himself up.

Dials phone number.

Be calm, be friendly don't get his back up.

Phone line ringing.

No answer. He's not in or he doesn't want to talk. He's turned the bell off so's not to hear me. No one wants to hear my side of it.

Only yesterday he wouldn't let me say a quarter of the things I had to tell him; I could hear him falling asleep on the end of the phone. It's disheartening. I'm perfectly reasonable, explain what I mean, prove it step by step, kidding myself he's following it all and then when I ask, 'What did I just say?' he doesn't know, cotton wool between the ears; Albert's the champion at that, but Tristan's not far behind, and as for Sylvie . . .

'Sylvie what did I just say?'

'You said if I'm messy with small things I'll be messy with big things and I've got to tidy my room before I can go out.'

. . . And the very next day she did not tidy it. When I make Tristan hear me out, he still can't come up with an answer.

'A boy needs his mother a mother can't do without her child it's perfectly obvious, even with the worst will in the world you can't deny that.' Well anyway he grabs the door, bolts downstairs four at a time leaving me shouting down the stairwell and I stop myself quickly in case the neighbours think I've gone mad; such a coward he knows I hate a scandal especially when I've already got an odd sort of reputation in the house, it's inevitable, their ways are so bizarre, some of it's bound to rub off on me.

Oh what the hell I broke my arse being so well-behaved Tristan loud mouth, couldn't care less, that vulgar laugh, I used to wish he'd drop down dead whenever he larked about with Sylvie in public.

Section VIII: I Must Defend my Untarnished Principles

Wind's up, it's like a tornado suddenly, how I'd love a great hurricane to sweep it all away, me with it; to plunge all together into oblivion. To die in a storm would give me some peace so long as no one's left behind to think about me.

I'm tired of fighting them.

Alas. I shan't get my typhoon I never do get anything I want. It's just a common little wind tearing down a few tiles and chimney pots. Everything's stingy in this world. I am the only one with grand dreams and I'd have done better to block them out.

Maybe I should stuff these things up my bum and get to bed. But I'm so wide-awake I'd only thrash about. If only I could have spoken to him on the phone, a pleasant chat, I'd be calm now. Wanker. Here I am with memories tearing me apart, so I call him and he doesn't answer. Don't slag him off don't start slagging him off that will wreck everything. I'm dreading tomorrow. I must be ready by four, I'll have hardly closed my eyes, I'll go down and buy petit-fours which Francis will tread into the carpet, he's bound to break the china, clumsy like his father, dropping ash everywhere and if I say anything Tristan explodes. He's never understood why it's so enormously important that I keep my house in good order. It's impeccable at the moment, this room, clean, gleaming, shining like the moon did once. By seven o'clock tomorrow night it will all be mucked up I'll have to do a major clean up, washed out though I'll be. It'll drain me explaining everything all over again from A to Z. He's so stubborn.

Stupid cow, fancy dumping Florent for him. We understood each other, me and Florent, he paid up, I lay back. Much cleaner than spinning all those yarns. But then it seemed like a great proof of love when Tristan offered to marry me and there was Sylvie, I wanted her to have a proper home and a respectable mother, married, a banker's wife. I broke my arse playing lady of the house befriending all the bores. It's not surprising I exploded from time to time.

'That's no way to handle Tristan,' Dédé said and then, 'I told you so.'

Tristan made me sick and he knew it. They don't like it when you tell them what you really think of them. They want you to believe their fancy words or at least pretend to. As for me I tear off the masks. I am still the little woman who says what she thinks and never cheats, and it makes my heart burn to hear him pontificating to all those prats on their knees in front of him. I'd like to stamp all the hot air out of them with my hob-nailed boots. Progress. Prosperity. Man's future. Humanity's happiness. Third World aid. World peace. I couldn't care less about Mankind, what has mankind ever done for me I'd like to know? I'm not going to cry for crazy bastards who massacre each other with bombs and napalm. Extermination.

Anyway, it makes the planet a little less crowded, and they all admit it's over-populated so what's the problem? If I was the earth all this vermin on my back would disgust me, I'd shake it off. I'd be happy to die so long as they all went with me. Why bother with children who mean nothing to me. My own daughter is dead and they've stolen my son.

Section IX: I've Got to be a Good Mother to Francis

I wish I'd won her back, I'd have made her into someone worthwhile. But it would have taken time. Tristan was no help, selfish pig, our rows bored him, he'd say, 'Leave her alone.' You shouldn't have children, Dédé's right in a way, they bring you nothing but grief. But if you've got one you have to bring it up properly. Tristan always took Sylvie's side: I could possibly have been in the wrong, but even if I was it's always disastrous if one of the parents undermines the other. He always supported her even when I was right. Take little Jeannie for instance, I melt when I think of her, all dewy-eyed, and adorable, a little girl can be so sweet, she reminds me of myself as a child; scruffy, neglected, slapped and scolded by that mother, the concierge, always trembling on the edge of tears, she thought I was lovely, she liked to stroke my furs, do little errands for me and I'd slip her some pennies when no one was looking, or some sweeties, poor wee girl. She and Sylvie were the same age; I hoped they'd be friends; Sylvie really let me down. 'Jeannie's so boring', she'd moan. I told her she had no heart, scolded her, punished her for it. Tristan defended her on the pretext that friendships don't happen to order, that went on for ages. I just wanted Sylvie to learn to be generous but in the end it was little Jeannie who gave up.

Footsteps, voices on the stairs (quieter), car doors.

Section X: I Must Face Things Head On

They've calmed down a bit up there. They've stopped dancing. I know what's happening they're all making love on feather beds or sofas, or on the ground, in cars; sick as a dog retching up all that turkey and caviare, it's unspeakable, I've a feeling I can smell vomit, I'd better burn some incense.

Finds incense, strikes match, lights it.

It's the gloomy hour.

The incense makes it smell like a funeral; candles flowers coffin: despair. Dead. Not possible. I stayed there sitting by her dead body for hours and hours thinking, 'But she'll wake up in a minute'. So much effort and struggle and drama and sacrifice all in vain.

Five years already. I can't bear it. Help I feel bad, too awful, get me out of here I don't want to break down again, no help me someone I can't take any more don't leave me alone. Who shall I call? Albert? He'd hang up straight away: he howls in front of the world, but tonight he's stuffed and merry and I'm the one left mourning. My mother? After all a mother is a mother, I didn't do her any harm, she's the one who mucked up my childhood, she's the one who insulted me, she's the one who had the nerve to say . . .

As she dials:

She has got to take it back I can't go on with that voice in my head, no girl can bear her mother's insults even if she is the ultimate whore.

The call is answered.

Is it really you on the phone? I'm amazed as well, but it had to happen in the end, because on a special night like this you're bound to be thinking of my grief and telling yourself that mothers and daughters can't stay enemies for life; especially since I can't really see why you ever blamed me . . . Don't shout, Mama.

Listens for a moment, then hangs up. Phone line burr.

She hung up. She wants peace. Am I supposed to ignore her poisonous tongue? Such hatred. She always hated me, she killed two birds with one stone by marrying me off to Albert.

She made sure of her fun and my misery. I didn't want to admit it, but it's blindingly obvious. She's the one who harpooned him in that exercise class and then she gobbled him up, old tart, stuffing her can't have been very appetizing but with all the men who've been through her she must know a trick or two. It's quite appalling the way these old biddies fuck. She was too old to keep him so she took advantage of me, laughing behind my back, then at it again. That day I got back early, she was all flushed.

My view is that you should have the decency to retire at fifty; I retired well before I went into mourning. It just doesn't interest me, I've got a block about it, I don't even dream about it any more. Old bag, I shudder to think what goes on between her legs, she stinks of scent but underneath she smells. Painting and powdering, never washed much, not what I call wash; when she pretended to take a shower it was just to show off her arse to Nanard, her son. Her son, her son-in-law. It makes you want to throw up. When you remarked they were paddling in shit they turned it around and said, 'You're the one with dirty feet.'

Section XI: I've Got to Get Out of This Cage

I know my dear little girl-friends would have loved to fool around with my husband, women are all tramps, but if I said a thing he turned it round and roared that I was contemptible. Jealousy is not contemptible true love has a beak and claws. I never did go along with sharing your partner. I wanted us to be a proper loving couple, I knew how to control myself but that doesn't mean I'm a wet blanket. No one eats me for breakfast. When I go over my past there is nothing to be ashamed of. But then I am the white blackbird.

Poor white blackbird, all alone. They want to shut you up in a cage. Shut in, done in. I'll end up dying of boredom really dying. I'm told that's what happens to newborn babies if no one takes an interest in them. The perfect crime, no trace left. That prat Tristan saying to me, 'Go on a trip you've got enough money.' Enough to travel in misery like that time with Albert; you won't catch me doing it again. I'm no snob I made Tristan see that luxury palaces full of women dripping with jewels and swanky doormen didn't excite me. But not seedy boarding houses and greasy spoons – oh no really! Smelly sheets, grubby tablecloths, sleeping in other folks' sweat, in their filth, you could catch lice or the pox, just the smell makes me sick; and that's not counting the way I get constipated to death because the very idea of following the rest of the world into those toilets blocks me up completely; the brotherhood of shit does very little for me.

And then what's the point of travelling alone? It was fun with Dédé; chic, two pretty girls in an open car, hair blowing in the wind; night-times in Rome, in the Piazza del Populo, we must have been a stunning sight.

But alone! What do you do on a beach, in a casino without a man? I had my fill of museums and ruins with Tristan. I'm not hysterical about broken columns or tumbledown shacks. I don't give two hoots for people from olden times they're dead that's their only advantage over the living but they were just as sickening in their own time. The picturesque does nothing for me – stinking filth, dirty washing, cabbage stalks, how pretentious to get excited . . .

. . . And they're the same everywhere, whether they're gobbling chips or paella or pizza, the same old bunch, a dirty bunch, the rich walk all over you, the poor want your cash, the old drivel on, the young fool around, the men show off, the women open their legs. I'd rather stay in my hole and read a thriller even though they're a pile of crap as well. Telly too what a load of rubbish. I was made for another planet I've missed my destination.

Section XII: I've Got to Be a Good Mother to Francis

Noises outside.

What do they think they are doing, carrying on right under my window.

Opens window.

What can they be talking about?

Young voices joking down below outside.

(*Calls out.*) Little creeps! (*Back inside.*) Brats in their mini-skirts and tights I hope they catch their death, what are their mothers thinking of? And look at those boys, hair down to their shoulders. Even from this distance they don't look very clean. If the police had an ounce of sense, they'd dump all those mangey beatniks in jail. The young; they take drugs, sleep around, don't respect anyone. I'm going to pour this water on their heads.

Takes bowl of water from make-up tray.

They could break my door down, smash my face in, I'm defenceless, I'd better close the shutters.

Rose's daughter, Danielle, was obviously one of them, and Rose played the big sister. They were never apart; thick as thieves, bum and shirt tail; and even though she kept a tight grip on her, and slapped her around from time to time, she never bothered to explain things to her. She was capricious and whimsical; I loathe that sort of person. Well, Rose is going to regret it later, I think; Dédé warned her right here, she said, 'One of these days Danielle will come home pregnant.'

I would have made Sylvie into such a good girl, I would have given her dresses and jewellery, I'd have been so proud of her whenever we'd gone out together. There's no justice in any of it; injustice, that's what's driving me mad. When I think of the mother I was; even Tristan acknowledged it. I made him see it, but even after that he said he'd do anything rather than leave Francis with me. Men don't make sense, they'll say anything and then they win by running away. Tristan bolting downstairs four at a time, leaving me screaming down the stairwell.

He shouldn't do it to me. I'm going to force him to be fair to me, I swear it as long as I live. He's going to have to give me my place at the hearth; I'll bring Francis up to be a good boy; then they'll see what sort of a mother I can be.

Section XIII: I've Got to Win Tomorrow

The sods are doing me in. Tomorrow's do will do me in. I've got to win I must I must I must I must I must. I'll do the tarot. No. If the cards are bad I'll chuck myself through the window; no I mustn't, those kids would only cheer me on. Think of something else, something jolly. That little fellow from Bordeaux. We didn't expect anything from each other, no questions, no promises, just jumped into bed and made love.

That went on for three weeks and then he went off to Africa, I cried and cried. That's cheered me up. Things like that only happen once in a lifetime: such a shame. When I go through it all in my head it seems to me I could have been an angel if someone had known how to love me. All those shits dumped me. They don't give two fucks, as far as they're concerned everyone could die in their holes; husbands cheat wives, mothers play around with sons, not a word spoken, lips sealed, such discretion.

I'm fed up with people being so two-faced. 'Your brother's really stingy' – as Albert kindly pointed out. I'm above such pettiness – but you know it's true – they always ate three times as much as us then squabbled about every little thing on the bill. And then Albert gave me a hard time about it, 'You shouldn't have told him what I said.' Down on the beach we had a huge row. Etiennette was crying, tears like lard running down her cheeks. 'Now he knows he'll change,' I said. I was a fool, I used to think they could change, that you could educate people by explaining things to them.

'Look Sylvie, just think about it. Do you know how much this frock costs? And how many times you'll be able to wear it? Let's put it back.'

Back to square one every time, I was exhausted. Nanard will be mean to the end of his days, Albert gets more and more elusive, lying, shifty and Tristan still just as pleased with himself, just as pompous. What a waste of time.

And when I tried to teach Etiennette how to dress Nanard bit my head off – 'Twenty-two and you're trying to turn her into an old maid' – so she carried on squeezing herself into those vulgar little frocks. And Rose shouting at me, 'you're being spiteful,' but I only told her out of loyalty. It's essential women stick together. What thanks did I ever get? I lent them money, interest-free, no one ever appreciated it, some even grumbled when I claimed it back. And you should have seen how quickly they vanished, all those people I'd helped, yet God knows I never took advantage of them. I'm not one of those people who thinks they can help themselves to everything, like Aunty Marguerite, 'Could you lend us your flat for the summer while you're on your cruise?' Bugger off! Hotels aren't there for decoration and if they can't afford a trip to Paris they'll just have to stay in their own holes. One's flat is sacred, I'd have felt violated.

It's like Dédé says, 'Don't let them eat you up'. But then she'd gladly swallow me whole. 'Haven't you got an evening coat you could lend me? You never go out'. I never go out but I used to, they're my frocks, my coats full of memories. I don't want some old cod wearing them instead of me. They'd smell afterwards. When I die, Mama and Nanard will share my belongings; oh no I want to live till the moths have eaten the lot, or else if I have got cancer I'll chuck them out. They've all taken advantage of me, Dédé most of all, drinking my whisky, showing off in my convertible. Lately she has been acting the big-hearted friend, but she didn't bother to call me tonight from Courcheval. When her husband's off and she's bored stiff sure then she drags her fat arse over even when I don't particularly want her to. But, tonight it's New Years' Eve and I'm all alone eating my heart out, she's out dancing and having fun and does she think of me? Does she fuck! No one ever thinks of me. As if I had been wiped off the face of the earth. Do I exist?

Pinches her arm frantically.

Ouch! I've pinched it too hard. I'll have a bruise.

No more cars, no more footsteps in the street, not a whisper in the house: silence. Like death. Like the mortuary.

It's so quiet.

Section XIV: I Must Relieve the Pain of Remorse

All my life it will be two o'clock in the afternoon on a Tuesday in June. 'Mademoiselle is so sound asleep I can't wake her.' My heart missed a beat I rushed in calling, 'Sylvie are you ill?' She looked as if she was asleep she was still warm. The doctor said, 'It's too late; she's already dead.' I screamed, I paced around the room like a lunatic, 'Sylvie, Sylvie why did you do this to me?' I can picture it now Sylvie so calm and relaxed and me like a caged animal, finding the little note for her father, it meant nothing I tore it up it was part of the act only an act I was sure I am sure – a mother knows her own daughter – she didn't mean to die she just got the dose wrong and she died, how terrible. It's all too easy to get hold of these drugs; these young girls feign suicide over nothing at all; Sylvie just followed the trend: she didn't wake up.

And they came they all kissed Sylvie none of them kissed me and in the midst of that paralysing silence Mama blurted out, 'You've killed her.' My mother, my own mother. They made her shut up but the expression on their faces, the silence the weight of their silence. Granted if I'd been one of those mothers who get up at seven in the morning she'd have been saved, but I live at a different rhythm, it's not a crime how was I to know? I was always there when she got back from school lots of mothers can't say as much. She was the one who shut herself in her room pretending to work . . . I never failed her. And, my own mother who abandoned me had the nerve to say that . . .

I had no idea how to answer her, her words were clanging round my head, I couldn't make any sense of it.

If only I'd kissed her that night when I came home . . . But then I didn't want to disturb her and she'd seemed almost cheerful earlier in the day. The agony of the next few days. I thought I would crack up at least twenty times.

School friends and teachers put flowers on her coffin without a single word to me; if a girl kills herself it's her mother's fault; that's how they saw it out of hatred for their own mothers. In at the kill. I almost let myself fall apart. I did fall ill after she was buried. All I could do was repeat, 'if only I'd got up at seven . . . if only I'd kissed her that night when I came in . . .' It felt as if the whole world had heard Mama condemn me. I didn't dare leave the house. I crept along by the walls, the sun thrust me in the pillory, I thought people were staring at me whispering pointing their fingers at me that's enough, enough I'd rather die on the spot than go through it again. I lost twenty pounds, I was a skeleton, lost my balance; reeled about. 'Psychosomatic', the doctor said, but Tristan still gave me the cash for the clinic. Such crazy questions I asked myself. I could have gone right over the edge.

Suicide attempt, she must have meant to screw things up for someone: but who? I should never have let her out of my sight, had her followed, asked questions, exposed whoever was to blame a boy or girl, maybe that slut of a teacher. 'No madame, there was no one special in her life', the sour bitch didn't give an inch, but if her looks could have killed me they would have; but they didn't fool me. I knew.

At her age, with things as they are, there must have been someone. Maybe she was pregnant or had fallen into the clutches of a dyke, or a pervert, blackmailing her abusing her threatening to tell me everything. Ah . . . I can't bear to imagine it. You could have told me everything Sylvie I'd have got you out of this sordid mess. It must have been a mess for her to have written to Albert. 'Papa forgive me but I can't take any more.' She couldn't talk to him, nor to the others they tried to wheedle it out of her but they were strangers. I was the only one she could have trusted. Without them. Without their hatred. Swines. You could have got to me, but you didn't. I'm not your scapegoat: I've shaken off your guilt. And your hatred doesn't frighten me I rise above it. Swines. They're the ones who killed her. They slung mud at me, set her against me, treated her like a martyr that suited her, all young people love to play the martyr; she took the part seriously, didn't trust me, wouldn't tell me a thing. Poor little sweetheart she needed my support, my advice. They deprived her of that, condemned her to silence, she didn't know how to get out of it by herself, she went on with the farce and the result was she died. Murderers! That's how they killed Sylvie my Sylvette my little love. I loved you. No mother could have worshipped you more: I only wanted what was best for you.

Takes out an album of photos.

All the different Sylvies. This child's face, a little bit drawn, this secretive adolescent. Looking deep into the eyes of this one, murdered at seventeen, I can honestly say, 'I was the best of mothers. You would have thanked me later.'

Section XV: I've Got to Win

I feel better for weeping and I'm starting to doze off. Don't fall asleep on the floor that'd fuck it up all over again. I'll pull myself together. Use the suppositories, get to bed. Set the alarm for noon so I'll have time to get ready. I've got to win. A man in the house again, my little boy to cuddle at bedtime, all this tenderness which never gets used. Then I really could get better.

What's this? I'm dropping off I'm relaxing. That'll be a smack in the mouth for them. Tristan's really somebody, people respect him. I want him on my side, then they'll have to treat me properly. I'm going to call him up, convince him right now.

She dials Tristan's number. He answers.

Wasn't it you who called me . . . ? Ah, I thought it was you. I'm sorry, were you sleeping – but I'm so happy to hear your voice. I've had a rotten night, nobody's shown any sign of life tonight even though they must know that parties are hard to take when you've suffered a great loss, all this racket and the lights have you noticed? Paris has never been as bright as it is this year they must have money to burn they'd do better to reduce the rates. I bury myself at home so I don't have to look at it. I'm too sad to sleep all by myself. I keep going over things in my mind. Listen I've got to talk it through with you as friends, without arguing, it's really vital I'm not going to get a wink of sleep until it's all sorted out.

You are listening aren't you? I've been puzzling over it all night well I didn't have anything else to do and quite honestly this situation is not normal, honestly we can't carry on like this, after all we are still married these two flats are such an expense you could sell yours for at least 20 million francs and I wouldn't disturb you, don't worry, there's no question of us restarting our married life, we're not in love any more. I'd shut myself up in the back room – don't interrupt – you can have all the girls you want, I don't care but since we're still friends there's no reason why we shouldn't live under the same roof. And we must for our son's sake. Just think about Francis for a moment. I've done nothing else all night long and I'm worn out. It's always bad for a child when his parents split up, they tell lies, they get complexes, they don't thrive. I so want Francis to thrive. You've no right to deprive him of a proper home . . .

But when we discuss it you always manage to wriggle out of it but this time I want you to hear me out. You're just being selfish. A bit of a monster. For no good reason. I don't have any vices, I don't drink or take drugs and even you admit I was a devoted mother . . . Well then? Don't interrupt. If you are thinking about your little flings I can only say again I'm not going to try and stop you.

It's not true that I'm impossible to live with, don't say I swallow you up, I don't wear you out. Yes I admit I've been a bit difficult, I explode from time to time, but that's just what I'm like, but if you had been patient and tried to understand me instead of sulking all the time . . . you're no saint, don't kid yourself, anyway what's done is done; you know perfectly well I've changed; I've suffered, I'm more mature; I can put up with things now I couldn't take before . . . Let me speak, you don't have to worry about rows we'll be civilized and the little one will be happy as he has a right to be I don't see what possible objection . . .

Why isn't this a good time to talk? It's the perfect time for me. You can give up five minutes sleep for me all the same I shan't get a wink until it's settled. Seven years now I've been rotting here like a leper. Let me speak – you owe me a lot you know, because you really haven't been very fair; you told me you were mad about me I gave up Florent and all my friends and then you turned your back on me; why did you ever say you loved me? Sometimes I think it was all just a bad joke. Yes, a bad joke; it's fucking unbelievable, one minute you adore me and the next you abandon me.

You hadn't realised what? Don't you dare go on about me marrying you out of self-interest I had Florent I could have had tons of others and if you must know being your wife wasn't such a dazzling prospect . . . And NO you are NOT Napoleon whatever you might think . . .

Don't say that again or I'll scream – you didn't say it but I can hear the words rolling around your mouth shut up, you've got it wrong, you've got it so wrong, I want to scream you made me believe you were crazy about me and I fell for it . . .

No don't say, 'Listen to me Murielle.' I know your version off by heart and stop looking so exasperated, that's right, exasperated. I can see you in the receiver. You've been even more of a let-down than Albert, he was young when we got married but you were forty-five, you should have taken your responsibilities seriously. Well all right you can't change the past. I promise not to go on about it. Let's forget it and make a new start. I can be sweet and gentle you know when people aren't too horrid. Come on tell me it's settled, we'll work out the details tomorrow. You sod! You're torturing me because I won't grovel but your airs and graces don't impress me and nor does your money.

Not for all the tea in China. We'll see about that. I'll talk to Francis, I'll tell him who you really are. And, what if I kill myself in front of him? That'd be a happy memory for him, wouldn't it? No it's not blackmail you thick bastard it wouldn't cost me much to do myself in. You shouldn't push people too far you don't know what they're capable of: some mothers even take the kids down with them.

Bastard! Turd! He's hung up . . .

Redials number.

He's not answering, he's not going to . . . bastard.

Sick, I'm so sick. I can't take any more. I'll go down to his place and cut my wrists and when they come back there'll be blood everywhere and . . .

She bashes her head against the wall.

I'll be dead. Ouch I've bashed it too hard I've cracked my skull. They're the ones who need the bashing. No I will not go mad they shan't get to me I'll stand up for myself. I'll find a way. But how? Bastards bastards. I'll have a heart attack, I must calm down.

Dear God! Please exist. Please let there be a Heaven and a Hell. I'll stroll through the groves of Paradise with my little boy and my darling girl and watch all the others writhing in the flames of envy. I'll see them all roasting and wailing and then I'll laugh. I'll laugh and laugh and the children will laugh with me.

Fade on **Murielle***'s laugh.*

The Woman Destroyed

I first came across Simone de Beauvoir as the writer of *The Second Sex* when I was a young actress and newly married in the late 60s. Both personally and professionally the book had a profound effect on me: I had not considered that my gender made any difference to my stance towards the world, and I had not considered what my motives might be in becoming an actress. I still find what she has to say there about women in love and the narcissism of women the most illuminating analysis I have yet read, and acknowledge a profound debt to her. Twenty years later I was delighted to be invited to contribute to a symposium on de Beauvoir at the ICA, and in the course of researching this event came across *The Woman Destroyed* for the first time.

Sandwiched between two novellas, the monologue shares with them a common theme: marriage and motherhood as a trap in which women of a certain age are cruelly and helplessly ensnared. Brought up with the expectation that love, marriage and babies are her destiny, Murielle finds herself at the age of 43 bereft of all three. She has no other resources; no skills, no confidence, (just a blind narcissistic arrogance), no sense that she might transcend her present lot through her own actions. As she says herself, she is stewing away in her own juice. There are many women like Murielle – and they are not, alas, all of an age where they can claim ignorance of what feminism teaches. Think of the average women's magazine, with its regular fodder of how to be attractive, sexy, a better home-maker, a more understanding mother or lover – not that I think these are bad goals in themselves. It's just that the emphasis continues to be on making oneself more desirable to someone else. The majority of women are still like Murielle: they seek to authenticate themselves by their value to someone else, rather than through their own action in the world.

I believe de Beauvoir wrote this piece as a morality tale; she claimed it came in response to the hundreds of letters she had received from her readers describing the confusions of their own lives. Whilst working on it, however, I came to believe that the violence of feeling in it could not have been created at second hand: rather that, as in all her writings, de Beauvoir had put herself into it. Thus my view of de Beauvoir has been profoundly changed by this piece. I no longer accept the rational, controlled person she presents in the autobiographical writings as the whole story. I am more and more convinced that the relationship with Sartre, which she called the crowning achievement of her life, was won at the cost of enormous denial on her part – denial of the very needs which Murielle trumpets so loud in this piece – to be nurtured, to be found sexually desirable, to be a mother, to not be lonely, to be allowed to be foolishly needy and loved despite it; to be saved from suicide.

She writes in huge periods, often with no punctuation. For the purposes of performance I have split up the text into shorter sentences and paragraphs, and added punctuation. I have also, with considerable help from my director, Vanessa Fielding, subdivided the monologue into fifteen sections, and given each a title which suggests an objective to play for that section. It would have been well-nigh impossible to orientate myself within the play without these objectives, and with them, the play becomes a series of hillocks which gradually ascend the mountain, instead of being one monstrous peak to scale. Certain objectives recur – to be a good mother for instance. In playing, we found that each section rises to a point of major release (of course there are other points of release within the sections) and that having played the major release it was then all right to take a moment's breather – both for one's own benefit and for the audience to catch up with the storm of words – before refocusing on the next objective and moving forward again.

A further thought came during rehearsal. I had done voice work some time back with a brilliant teacher, Kristin Linklater, in Massachusetts. She gave me back my voice after it had been traumatically damaged by an accident. In the course of that work, it became clear to me that all humans, as they live their life, go through a defensive process to survive, being fragmented by their own strong feelings which seem broadly to follow the same sequence.

This sequence goes, first, anger; then when that is stripped away, pain: and then finally a cathartic release of laughter. This is not the place to expand my reasons for believing this to be a universal pattern; what is relevant is that it seemed to be a useful structure to explore the broader sweep of Murielle's passage through New Year's Eve.

She is angry; violently, scatologically angry. At a certain point, having let out a lot of her personal demons, she begins to be able to look at the pain she is feeling and – I think – has never been able to acknowledge before tonight. That done, she at last attempts contact with the outside world – her estranged husband Tristan – a brilliant stroke, this, allowing us a glimpse of Murielle's more 'public' manner. When the conversation with Tristan doesn't work out, where can she turn? Only to laughter – briefly and, I admit, a laughter more than a little tinged with the desire for revenge – but laughter nonetheless. And it is the ability to laugh which, I believe, saves her from killing herself. She'll live to fight another day.

Diana Quick, 1993

Note on Music

The sound cues for *The Woman Destroyed* serve two purposes; the affirmation of realities in Murielle's situation i.e. noises *outside* the apartment, and a reflection of experiences which haunt her from within, notably the loss of her daughter.

It is consistent with the character's stream of thought that associations occur and re-occur, so that her mother, daughter, husband and self, etc. become united as one 'Fear'. Therefore we hear the musical repetition of a distorted 'child's-theme' as, ultimately, she returns to her childhood and experiences her horror with her own children.

While the music is at times strictly rhythmic, when combined with the actor's performance an aleatoric aspect to the overall relationship between actor and music is introduced. For example, it would not be realistic to anticipate exactly how long it will take to light the incense but rather than compete with the sound of the chiming bells, to keep with them, or wait for them, it is enough just to be aware of them as another thread in Murielle's mind leading naturally to the gloomy hour. The music is never used against the actor, it is a part of the actor's performance, as in the final lines of the play in which it is a real part of her dream of innocence – not a secondary expression of it, but a part of her being at that moment.

Brian Connor, 1993

Simone de Beauvoir was born in Paris on 9 January 1908 and died there on 14 April 1986. Her books include the novels *The Blood of Others* (1948)*, *She Came to Stay* (1949), *The Mandarins* (1957), *Les Belles Images* (1968), *The Woman Destroyed* (1969), *When Things of the Spirit Come First* (1982). Her non-fiction works include *The Second Sex* (1953), *Adieux: A Farewell to Sartre* (1984), *Letters to Sartre* (1991), and five volumes of autobiography: *Memoirs of a Dutiful Daughter* (1959), *The Prime of Life* (1962), *Force of Circumstance* (1965), *A Very Easy Death* (1966), *All Said and Done* (1974). She also wrote a play, *Les Bouches inutiles* (1945), not published in English.

Diana Quick starred at the National Theatre in *Phedra Brittanica* (John Dexter), *Plunder* (Michael Blakemore), *Troilus & Cressida* (Elijah Moshinsky), *Tamburlaine* (Peter Hall), and David Hare's *A Map of the World.* She has played at the RSC in *The Woman Pirates* and *The Changeling*, at the Lyric Hammersmith in *Fly Away Home* and Doug Lucie's *Progress* and in the West End musicals, *The Threepenny Opera* and *Billy.*

Her television credits are substantial and include *The Woman in White* (BBC), *Phantom of the Opera* (NBC), *Carianni and the Courtesans* (BBC), *Chekhov in Yalta* (BBC), *The Justice Game* (BBC), *Clarissa* (BBC), and most famously *Brideshead Revisited* (Granada). In 1994 she will be seen in *Dandelion Dead* (London Weekend) and *September Song* (Granada).

On film she starred in Michael Winner's *The Big Sleep*, Franklin Shaffner's *Nicholas & Alexandra*, Nagisha Oshima's *Max Mon Amour*, Desmond Davies' *Ordeal by Innocence*, Hugh Brodie's *1919*, Beban Kidron's *Vroom*, Michael Tuchner's *Wilt* and Roger Christian's *Nostradamus.*

* Dates are for first publication in Great Britain.

What Happened After Nora Left Her Husband

or

Pillars of Society

Elfriede Jelinek
English version by Tinch Minter

Characters

Nora Helmer
Personnel Manager
Women Workers
Eva
Foreman
Consul Weygang
Personal Assistant
A Gentleman
Secretary (male)
Government Minister
Annemarie
Torvald Helmer
Krogstad
Mrs Linde

The action happens in the twenties. Costumes should merely suggest time-shifts, especially into the future. But Nora must be played by an actress with acrobatic skills who can also dance. She must be able to do the gymnastics mentioned, but it doesn't matter if what she does seems professional or not – even to the point of looking a little ungainly. Eva must always come across as rather desperate and cynical.

What Happened After Nora Left her Husband received a rehearsed reading at the Goethe-Institut, London on 22 June 1992 with the following cast:

Stefanie Fayerman
Sally Edwards
Mark Lewis-Jones
Elizabeth Rothschild
Philip Whitchurch
Leo Wringer

Directed by Annie Castledine
Assistant Director Josie Sutcliffe

1

Personnel Manager'*s office. The* **Personnel Manager** *sits at a desk,* **Nora** *hangs around coquettishly picking up this and that, sits down a while, then suddenly jumps up and walks about. Her manner belies her rather dowdy clothes.*

Nora Left by my husband? No, I left him. I'm Nora from that play by Ibsen. To escape my muddle I'm going in for a vocation.

Personnel Vocations aren't an escape – they're a lifetime's commitment.

Nora I don't want to commit my life yet! I'm after wising up on myself.

Personnel Have you any professional experience?

Nora I've experienced caring for the elderly, the weak, the infirm, invalids and bringing up children.

Personnel We've no elderly, weak, infirm, invalids or children here. There are machines at our disposal.

Nora I'm disposing of the caring image – getting shot of it.

Personnel What about references?

Nora My husband would have written a reference for a good housewife and mother, if I hadn't boobed at the last moment.

Personnel We require references from outsiders. Don't you know any outsiders?

Nora No. My husband wanted a homebird, because a wife is never to look left or right but to concentrate on herself or her husband.

Personnel So he wasn't an employer in the legal sense, like me.

Nora He was an employer! In a bank. Let me give you a tip – don't let your position harden your heart like he did.

Personnel The lonely life at the top always makes men hard-nosed. Why did you jack it in?

Nora I wanted to develop in a job from an object to a human being.

Personnel We only employ human beings; some are more human than others.

Nora Before I could become human I had to leave my husband.

Personnel Lots of our female manpower would give an arm and a leg for a home. Why did you leave your place?

Nora Because I knew my place.

Personnel Can you type?

Nora I can do office work and embroidery, knitting and sewing.

Personnel Who have you worked for? Name, address, telephone number.

Nora A private company.

Personnel Private isn't public. First go public then you can jack in being an object.

Nora My special knack is for unconventional jobs. I've always held conventions beneath contempt.

Personnel What makes you believe such unconventionality is on the cards?

Nora I'm a woman full of complicated biological processes.

Personnel And your qualifications for what you call unconventional?

Nora I'm gentle and I'm artistic.

Personnel Then you must go for a further marriage.

Nora I'm gentle and I'm rebellious, I'm not a simple personality, I'm many-faceted.

Personnel Then don't go for a further marriage.

Nora I'm still out for myself.

Personnel (*breaking in*) Sound lungs, eyes? Dental defects? Sensitive to draughts?

Nora No. I've looked after my body.

Personnel Then you can start at once. Any further qualifications that didn't occur to you just now?

Nora I haven't eaten a thing for days.

Personnel How unconventional!

Nora I want to be conventional, but only for the time being till I get the hang of being unconventional.

2

Factory, shop floor, **Women Workers, Eva** *and* **Nora** *at work.*

Worker Got any children?

Nora Yes. And everything in my blood cries out for them. They are my blood. But my brains tell me I come first – *before* my children.

Worker Working with people – in textiles – gets into women's blood. But we've got to let this blood out.

Eva Blood disorders are a common occupational disease here.

Worker At work our thoughts drift off to our husbands and kids, they're what's real.

Eva Machines are unreal.

Nora Well stop then. Go for your own self-image, your future – it may be somewhere else. I risked taking that step.

Eva My future might be poker work, Indian temple dances. How would I know?

Nora By going all out for it. By looking into yourself, then acting on what you see.

Worker My future's the kids, but because I work in a factory I never have enough time for them.

Nora Sometimes you've got to leave the lot without looking back.

Eva She overlooked the detail of her kids starving without her.

Worker Nora, how could you leave your little ones so vulnerable?

Worker You must have left a bit of your heart at the same time!

Worker We're just ordinary women, we'd never have been up to that.

Nora But I'm complicated and was up to that.

Worker Without our kids we can't dream that something better will come through the kids some time.

Nora It costs me dear – I'm cut up inside – not having my children.

Eva The machine might kill, then you'd be cut up even more.

Nora Urgh, how grisly!

Worker We can be thankful it hasn't grabbed us yet.

Eva We'd give the world for a man's hand and after that we'd happily swap the machine for the hand.

Nora But sooner or later every couple heads into a crisis.

Worker No time for that.

Worker Only the middle classes have got time for that.

Eva Anyway, when a period of economic instability looms in the form of unemployment, they pick women off the machines.

Worker Then childbirth will be a creative experience again.

Eva Hearth and home will be something again.

Worker And finally the law will allow us to give up our wedding rings like you, Nora.

Eva We'll give gold for iron.

Nora Only give up your ring because deep inside your husband feels like a stranger again.

Worker We don't know about all that. That's for the middle classes.

Eva First gold for iron, then children for the front line.

Worker Think of it, even mothers radiating beauty again.

Eva It'll soon be here, the time's drawing near.

Nora I'll never get used to the machines. And I'll never get used to women and men being on different levels. That's something else we've got to fight!

Worker That's for the middle classes.

3

Factory, changing room, lockers etc. **Nora, Eva,** *the young* **Foreman**.

Foreman I love you Nora. As soon as I realised you're the best catch right now, I knew I loved you.

Nora I'm pushing thoughts of love away. Love doesn't care about value because it isn't just out for itself. But I am going all out for myself.

Foreman I'm all out for me too, I want you for me.

Eva Why don't you want me? I do everything for you!

Foreman I don't want what's offered to me, I want what costs the earth.

Eva I've been here for years, and you don't love me.

Foreman Nora's femininity hasn't been crushed by standing too long at the machine. Nora's more of a woman than you.

Eva Well, I get more in my pay packets.

Nora There's no time for love, there's only time for self-discovery.

Eva If you can't love me then get your brains round this – they're shifting production, not renewing machinery and letting our housing fall down around us!

Foreman Women grow hard if their emotions aren't returned. It shouldn't come as a surprise that I don't return your love.

Eva If we didn't brighten up our houses with window-boxes, the lack of repairs would be screamingly obvious.

Foreman There's not a glimmer of feeling in you.

Nora 'The vast majority of people are supposedly so effeminate that their thoughts and actions are not determined by level-headed judgements but by sentiment.' Adolf Hitler.

Eva Beside the point now.

Foreman I love listening to you, Nora. I don't follow the words, as your voice is music. Music for the reason that feelings enhance a woman.

Eva But *I* love you.

Foreman What's that to me?

Eva Can't you see our flats are falling down? Crumbling amongst the vases, lace curtains and garden gnomes? Or have you only got eyes for Nora? You really should have been a . . .

Nora (*breaking in*) We must show solidarity, put jealousy aside, Eva. Women's nature gives us a strong inner togetherness.

Foreman When you love someone, you don't notice any corruption. You can't love me as much as you claim, Eva.

Nora How can you let him walk all over your pride, Eva?

Eva In love we all swallow our pride.

Nora I never could. But still I do want you as a friend. Do you, Eva?

Eva You can afford to be generous!

Foreman I want Nora. I want Nora.

Eva I love you!

Foreman I don't want you, I want Nora.

Nora I don't love you.

Foreman You only think that because you don't know what it's like when someone loves me.

4

Nora *sweeping the factory floor, the* **Foreman** *sits there, watching her, grabbing hold of her now and then but* **Nora** *always disentangles herself, the* **Personal Assistant** *comes on.*

P.A. I've a message for you: tomorrow afternoon our Personnel Manager is taking some gentlemen from a friendly syndicate round the plant. As a woman you're to have an earlier free hour to get things cleared up – not forgetting the toilets, please.

Nora It takes me all my time clearing up as it is.

P.A. And the Board of Directors wants you to produce a programme of a cultural nature by way of welcome. As I'm informed, Mrs Helmer, you have a gift for these things, or should I say practical experience. They say you once moved in circles where culture meant something, as is still partially apparent. So, one or two songs for mixed choir without an orchestra, please, a sort of beanfeast of yesteryear, then maybe a short dance piece, which I'll leave to you.

Nora You're a woman, aren't you?

P.A. Of course. Isn't it obvious?

Nora Why don't you look like a woman, more cheerful? Why do you look so serious?

P.A. When one's a director's P.A. one doesn't need one's lips in a fixed grin because one's own life is fine without that.

Nora Don't you feel any bond with me?

P.A. At best we're bonded by birth pains, if we ever have children. But I'd probably be more sensitive to those pains.

Goes.

Nora I could dance the tarantella tomorrow. My husband taught me.

Foreman Don't dance the tarantella. It would only widen the gulf between us.

Nora If anyone else can dance the tarantella, she's more than welcome. Apart from me no one can do a thing.

Foreman The works choir's all but professional!

Nora Tomorrow after my dance I'll just slip out of your life. Now these weeks are over, a little voice is telling me I can't go on without my children. This long ordeal has shown me that.

Foreman You mustn't do that, Nora! You mustn't go! Work isn't always a pain or an ordeal.

Nora I'm at breaking point.

Foreman By dancing you'd stand out so sharply against the background – that's me – I wouldn't be seen any more.

Nora I can't stand it here any more. I must go to my children – they are waiting for me. I'll live all the more for my little ones now, to make up for my failings.

5

Manager*'s office. As the* **Personnel Manager** *makes a speech,* **Consul Weygang** *and another* **Gentleman** *talk quietly to each other, they are obviously the centre of attention. Upstage two or three others, a secretary etc.*

Personnel Consul Weygang, you've become one of our country's foremost business figures. You foster the community as textile king, as President of the Olympic Company, of the League for the Protection of World Nature, of the Society for the Furtherance of Alpine Studies, as a member of the Council for Development Policy at the Ministry for Economic Cooperation and of the Treasury's Foreign Trade Council.

Weygang (*quietly*) As President of the Wholesale and Import-Export Federation, I've squared my position most agreeably with the short-term financial difficulties of my firm.

Gentleman I do remember, Weygang, from your powerbase as the kingpin of an organisation representing twelve states as well as about 75 trade associations – roughly 100,000 firms – you went all out for these 14.5 million citizens securing the rural district's interest and so on, in a speculative cotton deal with Egypt. A perfect squaring of position and enterprise.

Weygang The future lies in synthetics so I've no further interest in natural fibres.

Gentleman What's the purpose of this visit? Has the Minister . . .

Weygang *goes 'psst', the* **Gentleman** *continues more quietly.*

Gentleman Has the Minister still not cast an eye over the deeds? You know . . .

Personnel . . . you serve a further five supervisory or rather executive committees, among others the Bräuning Brewery, the Herdy Bank and the State Credit Institute for Industrial Construction.

Weygang *and the* **Gentleman** *have retreated to the window, speaking very quietly.*

Gentleman How far do you think it's leaked out that this whole area's up for grabs . . .

Weygang There's talk of recent unrest in the work force, because the machinery gets more obsolete by the day, you know . . . then the housing . . . of course, no one's chipping in with further funds.

Gentleman People are getting worried.

Weygang The beauty is, you know, the other party . . . our friend who still owns the thing, isn't interested in investing. The factory's been unlettable for ages, no transport infrastructure . . .

Gentleman Of course you'd relocate production.

Weygang But there again, if we're too interested in the area now they'll get the wind up, don't forget.

Gentleman But there again, if they want to sell to us, the works must be seen as a going concern.

Weygang But there again, no one must winkle out what certain interested circles are really . . .

Gentleman The energy debate's over . . .

Weygang Yes, the future is in energy. I always so admired Hugo Stinnes . . . ! Amalgamating Siemens-Schuckert's electricity trusts with the Rheinelbe coal and iron supplies into that massive supercartel . . .

Gentleman At that time weren't you going after currency deals too?

Weygang I wasn't on the first rung at that time. As you know, he bought foreign exchange with Marks borrowed from the Reichsbank, so the Mark fell through the floor.

Gentleman He could then pay back the loan at a fraction of the original rate.

Weygang And the little people took the money for their day-to-day shopping round in wheelbarrows.

Gentleman Those were the days!

Weygang They'll be with us again.

Gentleman This time you'll see to it they're with us again.

Weygang *does a pantomimic 'psst', takes him by the shoulder and leads him back to the front row without another word. Having emptied a glass, the* **Personnel Manager** *goes on.*

Personnel . . . awarded the sash of the Grand Order of Merit, given the freedom of your home town, the big silver seal of honour of the . . .

Weygang *is about to go out of the door and the* **Gentleman** *about to follow, but* **Weygang** *indicates he's to stay and keep the others occupied. The* **Gentleman** *complies with a wink and reassuring gestures.* **Weygang** *goes off alone and furtively.*

6

Factory interior. It's been tidied and basically smartened up with garlands, Chinese lanterns, flowers, sprigs etc. Upstage perhaps two or three simple tables laid for the workers' gala. Downstage **Nora** *practising the tarantella. She dances. After a while the* **Personnel Manager** *comes in.*

Personnel Why are you here so early?

Nora I can't dance later on if I don't do a dress rehearsal first.

Personnel Don't be so wild. Better to go for more in your paypackets!

Nora That's how it has to be.

Dances even more wildly.

Personnel You could make your steps more sensual, not so bland.

Nora I'm not in a night club or cabaret. I'm on my own here doing my workmates a favour.

Personnel By dancing you're doing the firm a favour rather than your workmates.

Nora But that's the same! Cooperation's what counts.

Personnel Dance more sexily.

Nora (*breathless*) My husband said it was indecent, if I danced too wildly.

Personnel Did your husband pay you? Well then. We pay you handsomely.

Nora Not any more! I'll soon be going back where I come from, where I fit in better.

At the back **Weygang** *comes in unnoticed, stops abruptly and observes – but unobserved – as* **Nora** *dances.* **Nora** *dances more wildly, weaving in acrobatic tricks, making a big bridge.*

Personnel Stop, watching you has made me giddy! It must hurt you.

Nora *goes on dancing.*

You'll break something!

Nora *goes on dancing. At last,* **Weygang** *comes forward and with a gesture shoos away the* **Personnel Manager**, *who bows low and goes off.*

Weygang God, what a figure the woman's got! Without figures like that in our lives we'd never bother with reproduction.

Nora (*who has still not noticed him*) I'll run through the steps once more the way my husband taught me, sensually, but not too sensually.

Weygang (*quietly*) What's too fast or wild for some is just right for me. Where feeble or fearful fellows flinch I'm drawn on by magic.

Nora *goes on dancing, suddenly sees* **Weygang** *and is startled.*

Nora Who are you?

After a short pause, goes on dancing. **Weygang** *says nothing.*

Nora It seems you're not only looking at my body but at my soul. I sensed that at once. No one's looked at my soul for ages.

Weygang It's as if lightning's crashing inside me. How come?

Nora (*dancing*) It's the harmony of the body and what's within, isn't it?! Many men hardly ever notice the inner woman.

Weygang I am aware of the whole you. An arrow's suddenly shot through me. Isn't this a feeling I thought I buried ages ago?

Nora If something's gripping you with the power of an obsession, don't fight it.

Weygang Even I must have a private life sometime.

Nora May I dedicate this innocent little dance to you?

Going on dancing the whole time, like a matador, **Nora** *tosses him her scarf.*

Weygang I grab it, and accept it as a sacred duty. Now dance just for me!

Nora I'll forget the whole world and dance just for you. I don't know you but you seem so near, so familiar to me. Lightning's crashing inside me too.

Weygang Lightning's flashing all the more now.

Nora All of a sudden you're showing a hint of impurity in your thoughts. I'm not shying away from this look, but tingling under it. I'm facing up to something new.

Weygang Can't I look at my newest, most precious possession?

Nora But surely you own many, much more precious possessions?!

Weygang Naturally. But they're valueless in comparison with you.

Nora Words like that make a woman bloom. They're words I've done without for ages.

She dances nearer to him, suddenly snuggling up to him.

Weygang You've still got the tarantella in your blood, I see. And that makes you even more of a temptress.

Nora (*dancing away once more*) I'm trying one last time to escape those invisible threads. Please don't say a word! Let's share this silence.

She comes into **Weygang**'s *arms.*

Nora This fur reminds me of something I've done without for ages.

Weygang What's your name?

Nora Nora.

Weygang Like the main character in Ibsen's play?

Nora You know everything . . . You're so powerful!

Weygang Even men can be shocked by powerful feelings. You're no ordinary worker. You're something else.

Nora I can only put up a weak fight. You give off such power.

Upstage **Women-Workers** *in their Sunday best come on and form themselves into a choir. And a few male workers at the back for the low voices. They wait like statues for their entry.*

Weygang You're dancing as if it's a matter of life and death; that must be because I am what matters, huh?!

Nora I'll do a cartwheel and the splits as a finishing touch.

Does so.

Then I'll straighten up again, groaning and weary, but happy.

Does so.

Weygang Now I can't go on fighting shy of my feelings.

They embrace. The **Workers** *quietly begin to hum. The* **Foreman,** *unable to endure it any more, bursts out of the choir towards* **Nora.**

Weygang Nora, come with me!

Nora I can't go on saying no. I'm saying yes!

Foreman (*shaking* **Nora**) Nora, you can't just go! You don't even know the man!

Nora (*taking no notice of him*) I must yield to his magnetism.

Weygang (*taking no notice of the* **Foreman**) Thank you. I'll take care of you.

Foreman You mustn't leave me, Nora! You can't just go off with a stranger.

Nora I love him.

Foreman It's his money you love.

Nora Money was a dreadful letdown for me once, this time it'll give me lift-off. This time I'll keep money and love apart.

Weygang Are we going, my love? Let me lead you to my limousine.

Foreman But what if I can't live without you, Nora?

Nora Life always goes on.

Weygang Come on! A whole for ever after is ahead of us.

Manager (*timidly*) There's still our little cultural programme . . .

Weygang *and* **Nora** *stand wrapped round each other, while the* **Workers** *keep humming the opening bars.*

Nora Oooh please, darling! I'm to sing the soprano solo! It'd make me so happy!

Weygang If my boisterous little bumblebee really wants to . . .

Nora Please, please . . . to sweeten it for you I'll do endless standing jumps.

Does so.

Weygang Then of course I can't say no. It gives life a brand new feel.

Nora *goes into the midst of the choir singing with the others a church-bell waltz,* ding dong ding dong. *As they sing*:

Weygang Business doesn't depend on natural forces with inevitable results but on efficient people doing their jobs. They must be regulated to stop them opening the door to chaos and anarchy.

The stage slowly darkens. The choir goes on singing in the darkness: Oh, how happy I am in the evening – *in canon.*

7

Factory visit. **Women-Workers** *sitting at the machines giving a demonstration for the visitors. The dialogue alternates between the two groups.* **Nora** *has* **Weygang**'*s coat on, he has his arm round her shoulder and fondles her now and then.* **Nora** *nods showily to* **Weygang**'*s words.*

Eva (*quietly*) Something's casting a shadow. Could it be the shadow of speculation?

Worker I'm often so weary, so worn out I can't even read or write. What employer ever cares about his workers' souls or knowhow?

Worker Still, in spite of work, I long to be a human being, to live like one.

Eva Then take the plunge, fall in love and all shadows will vanish – there'll be just love, pure and simple.

Worker You'd need to glam up a bit, take more care of yourself . . .

Eva But then we might fall into the cutting-out blade or the carding machine, or the shredder might hack us to pieces . . .

Worker Mustn't get too obviously mutilated. A shred of femininity must be preserved.

Worker Our husbands are cheered up by beating us up when we can't console them about their conditions.

Worker No man's so low he's got nothing lower: a wife.

Weygang (*loudly*) Society stands or falls with the state of marriage.

Gentleman Some women are the safe-keepers of our homes so in their turn they enjoy being totally kept by us, the others are trash.

Weygang A man can overcome middle-class morality, provided he is middle-class.

Gentleman . . . Man overcomes middle-class morality by destruction, struggle, robbery and violence.

Weygang Even a woman's brains can kickstart our desire. To tell the truth the best kick men get is from conquering women's little brains.

Worker (*quietly again*) A proud, solemn man would bend over us, wipe away our blood with his white handkerchief, wrap us in soft kashmir blankets and carry us to his limo.

Eva This kind-hearted soul won't even mind spots of blood on his snow-white leather upholstery.

Worker He wouldn't be a gigolo – I've heard all about them.

Eva He'd have to be going dirt cheap, or we'd never get him!

Worker Better if he's gone off through age than impotence, physical handicap, or a weak mind or character.

Worker I'd far rather have a young . . .

Worker Youth won't get you anywhere.

Worker Well I'm young.

Eva Rather young and rich than poor and old.

Worker Impotence wouldn't put me off.

Worker His looks wouldn't put me off, because all that counts are love and good nature.

Weygang (*loudly again*) Sexual drive does not reside in pure women. Love alone abides there. Woman's natural desire is to satisfy a man.

Gentleman Sad to say, women often ruin themselves at work deliberately.

Worker (*quietly again*) Mental handicap's OK by me. You can always make up for it by love, dedication and patience.

Worker A nice character's all I'm after. Don't need good looks for that. He's not to drink.

Worker You've all got men. But I'm free! Free for him!

Eva Impotence might be a perk. No more kids to be dumped on you.

Worker Where there's money, what's a few kids?

Worker Only his nature counts.

During the **Women**'*s last speeches the employers' delegation departs.* **Weygang,** *who has inspected everything, now takes* **Nora** *with him, leaving the* **Workers** *behind.*

8

The house of the businessman **Weygang**. *Study.* **Weygang**, *the* **Minister**, **Weygang's Secretary**, *who stays upstage.*

Weygang Well, my dear Minister, what do you say to Nora's body?

Minister I can hardly credit what I've heard, that she's already had various children.

Weygang Actions speak louder than words.

Minister Some even louder than others.

Weygang Business mustn't take measures for the world as it should be, and isn't, but for helping the world as it is.

Minister Or as that Socrates so brilliantly put it: I know that I know nothing, ha ha . . .

Weygang And he added: But you don't even know that, ha ha . . .

Minister One either knows or one doesn't know.

Weygang Knowledge is power.

Minister Nothing at all is nothing at all.

Weygang It may well mean the rumours are true.

Minister Which rumours?

Weygang You know what I mean. I've inspected the plant. I must admit they're trying to give the impression – however amateurish – of a firm with a healthy infrastructure.

Minister And is it healthy or isn't it?

Weygang Sick as a dog. Transport costs have been too high for ages. There are plans to relocate. But there must be someone who's got an interest in palming the whole lot off on me.

Minister So far as I can gather a majority of the board of trustees want to close it, then wait quietly in the hope that the site's value will pick up.

Weygang We can't wait so long, as you know. I hope you know! I must discover that link in the chain with an interest in selling.

Minister There's always a weak link, as Nature's countless wonders show.

Weygang He's not yet mine but he will become mine, once you get me the information, just as Nora became mine.

Minister That's some woman . . .

Weygang My Nora, my sunshine, my dearest possession.

Minister . . . could as easily be my sunshine.

Weygang She's not just a face and body, she's got a remarkably broad education.

Minister You're a good businessman Fritz, I'll give you that. You know how to sell.

Weygang The thought of parting with her is like a dagger cutting right through me.

Minister This old hand says: to the mythic woman – her skin, her body – the shrine of eternal contradictions!

Weygang But still – capital's the great beauty of all time!

Minister She's all childlike innocence, like – let's say – Wedekind's Lulu. She has no moral criteria.

Weygang Yes. I love her, I'm absolutely addicted to her.

Minister I could love her too.

Weygang Nature favours business on a grand scale, just as she favours love like mine for Nora. The usual Swiss accounts?

Minister Yes. But this time you must put something in, dear fellow.

Weygang What for?

Minister I'm not a little excited by your Nora.

Weygang I'll never trade in the woman I love, I'd sooner trade in my right arm – or myself.

Minister Then you won't?!

Weygang Nora and I will be Darby and Joan sharing a ripe old age.

Minister It's not a ripe old age I fancy sharing with her.

Weygang Yes well, in my experience everlasting passion only lasts a short while. Wait for my passion to die and she's yours.

Minister Done.

Weygang Losing Nora will be like knives cutting my heart.

Minister You won't be parting with her gratis. Three borough councils are after the deal, and I've got them in my pocket.

Weygang Fine, let's say three weeks. Capital's *the* great beauty.

Minister What we're discussing will be built on the site in question. You know yourself the site's ideal: thinly populated, cooling water galore, long approach roads for Joe Public's rallies, no industry to speak of, etc. etc.

Weygang Is it all tied up? You have read the small print?

Minister And the local mayor's all for it.

Weygang Good.

Minister Come the spring the site's value will have grown ten times. Could be more.

Weygang The Accounts Bank is principle shareholder, yes? And the Accounts Bank has its weak link.

Minister Very true.

Weygang Thank you, Minister, for our little chat.

The **Minister** *puts on sunglasses and goes out by a side-door.* **Weygang** *turns to his* **Secretary** *who immediately puts aside the papers he's been sorting all this time.*

Weygang By the way, do you know what the Minister doesn't know? Who one of the Accounts Bank Directors is?

Secretary No, Mr Weygang.

Weygang Helmer.

Secretary I don't know a Helmer.

Weygang But you know a Nora. She was married to him.

Secretary Unbelievable, Mr Weygang.

Weygang He got his position by pulling strings, he hasn't a bean nor a bond to his name. I'm told he's unbelievably ambitious, lives well beyond his means. And they say he's getting married again, this time to a young socialite.

Secretary I never did, Mr Weygang.

Weygang Good thing the Minister hasn't picked that up, or he'd neatly double his cut.

Secretary How come, Mr Weygang?

Weygang If he then informs Helmer . . . could force the price sky high . . .

Secretary Oh God, Mr Weygang!

Weygang I must get Helmer to sell without getting suspicious – that might not be so tricky as he wants to sell anyway.

Secretary All the better, Mr Weygang.

Weygang I'll set Nora to scent him out. She'll squeeze all we need out of him.

Secretary That sounds plausible, Mr Weygang.

Weygang Now I've shown her the good life, she wants revenge on Helmer for systematically keeping her from the good life.

Secretary I never did, Mr Weygang.

Weygang And I've almost wiped out her narrow-mindedness, broadened her horizons remarkably. It's a beautiful, wild, broad, wanton, mad world!

9

***Nora**'s luxury boudoir.* ***Annemarie** tidying up.* ***Nora** dances in through the door, wearing an elegant negligé.*

Nora It's going to be so wonderful Annemarie, I can see it now!

Annemarie At last my madam Nora's coming back to her essential duty! I always say: you can lose a man, but the children stay with you.

Nora I'm not going to lose this man, my old Annemarie!

Annemarie They'll be over the moon, having their little mother again. I don't dare think about it, but Nora, suppose you are expecting a sweet secret soon . . .? Suppose you're expecting a fourth . . .?

Nora I've only just become a woman, I want to enjoy that now, not have another child straight away . . .

Annemarie Women shouldn't speak like that – it's a sin against the children . . .

Nora Run along Annemarie, that'll be the master!

***Weygang** comes in,* ***Annemarie** goes out,* ***Nora** throws herself into* ***Weygang**'s arms.*

Nora Darling, I feel my love for you getting stronger and stronger! The force of my feelings shocks me, and makes me so feminine.

Weygang You mustn't be shocked, my little one! If you are shocked, be shocked at the ageing process ahead of you.

Nora My darling's such a joker . . . sometimes against men and women together, or just one of them. When it's against a woman alone it's not funny because women take it harder.

Weygang That's your high spirits – they're always bubbling out. Most women are so deep, but men can be shallow, empty, trivial. Life grinds men down more because they love more passionately than women.

Nora To tease you the little girl looks at the door and asks what nice game we're going to play today.

Weygang Today for once I must talk seriously with my little girl.

Nora Ooooh, slightly offended I stamp my foot and spin round on my toes glancing archly from below to show I'm not as serious as I seem.

Weygang Now, now, my lark mustn't let her wings droop.

Nora I hit the table with my little fist, look up to you through my tousled curls with anxiety, fear and the sweet certainty of being loved.

Weygang Love turns serious at last after all these months.

Nora Yes, our love's become deeper now, more mellow. It makes one meek and serious.

Weygang Has my little bird been squandering her nest-egg again?

Nora The rogue in you sparkles through this seriousness. Impetuously I dance round the room, fluttering my negligé's wide sleeves.

Weygang Could my woodlark bear responsibility? Be a true partner to me? Women as partners are becoming increasingly fashionable.

Nora But I'm more of an old-fashioned woman, happy to play second fiddle to my man.

Weygang Then I'd better hold my peace . . .

Nora No, tell me, tell me!

Weygang Better not! . . . Maybe I really should go for a partner . . .

Nora Tell me! Tell me! Now I'll do a perfectly formed arabesque.

Does so.

Weygang A capitalist makes more from his money without producing.

Nora . . . as he shares everything equally with me, both joy and sorrow come back to him doubled in love, ha ha!

Weygang My lark's going to burst with laughter.

Nora Support the man in his business deals! It's far better to have a man who deals on his own and doesn't need support.

Weygang It's a very big transaction, Nora. That's why I'm so serious.

Nora Such seriousness is like a hammer. You feel so safe under it.

Weygang Your former husband Helmer is tangled up in it, you know.

Nora (*laughing in disbelief*) No!

Weygang Capital can also cut loose and run wild.

Nora (*abrupt and serious*) I'm not duty-bound by friendly feelings for Helmer, you know.

Weygang So you could run wild over your petty feelings?

Nora What?

Weygang It's to do with a real big time speculation.

Nora Do your own dirty work! If women didn't hold you back . . . with our tiny hands . . .

Weygang I must make him do what I want while he believes I'm doing what he wants.

Nora I'm only a weak woman, I can't make anything submit to me, but I submit to you.

Weygang Your physical features that once attracted me can also attract others . . .

Nora Come off it, donkey!

Weygang Well I've invested quite a bit in you. Investment implies a quantity of goods with one thing in common: they aren't directly used.

Nora But you've used me, donkey! And it was so lovely! I do everything for you except one thing.

Weygang Sometimes one must wound oneself. Sometimes a woman sees that when a man wounds her badly it's proof of his love. Because in doing that he wounds himself far more.

Nora No!

Weygang What would the careless little bird lose if she squandered everything?

Nora Her nest-egg.

Slowly grasping it.

Weygang Next week's motto: no squandering, but giving of oneself.

Nora But I've given a lot . . . and of myself.

Weygang I give a lot too: myself plus added value.

Nora You can't expect that from me.

Weygang If you begged your baby donkey prettily now for something you passionately . . .

Nora Then . . .

Weygang Your donkey would leap about and play all sorts of cheerful tricks, if you were affectionate and submissive.

From now on **Nora** *is silent,* **Weygang** *does her part in an assumed voice.*

Weygang You will do it, won't you? I've got to know what it's about first. About a railway network – like that other Ibsen play, *Pillars of Society*. Railway! Why a railway? Well, we don't own the site in question yet. No, why not? We've got to buy it first! You shouldn't keep buying when you've already got what matters most – love. Then the world will just hurtle into oblivion and only our love will be left. The world can hurtle away once the deed of purchase is settled. But still, I'm sorry for the people working there now, as it is. You're always thinking of others when you should be thinking only of me. Most of the time I do think only of us. We're setting up another place, as it is, a new estate which we'll call the Nora-Helmer-Towers . . . bright, friendly flats . . . the first fitted kitchens in the history of publicly assisted home-building . . . perhaps even . . . I hardly dare say it out loud – it is rather a mouthful . . . the Nora-Weygang-Towers!!! The Nora-Weygang-Towers! Did I hear right darling? Actually I only heard the two words Nora and Weygang.
I answer: yes, perhaps!
Oh, darling!
I answer even more positively: yes who knows?! So honestly it isn't horrid, what I want to do there? No.
And you're honestly going to crown our union by marriage? Yes possibly.
Oh, darling at last I really and truly belong to you.
That's how it is with possessions, my little lark.

He embraces **Nora**, *who stands there frozen. He looks at her a long while smiling, before he goes out.*

10

Nora*'s bedroom,* **Annemarie, Nora**.

Annemarie Your expression has gone so soft, Nora, it tells me you've been thinking about your essential duty . . .

Nora Thinking? Me? Right now a woman is turning her back on a social system, in this case the family.

Annemarie Don't snap the invisible threads binding you to the children!

Nora (*picking up some knitting from a chair*) This your knitting?

Annemarie Rough words don't suit your sweet nature.

Nora So you knit?

Annemarie You've been a mother for years, Nora, but you're still an empty-headed, irresponsible tomboy . . .

Nora You know what, you'd be better embroidering.

Annemarie They're innocent mites. I once had to part with an innocent mite . . .

Nora It looks far prettier. Now look: you hold the embroidery like this in your left hand, then take the needle in your right . . . like this . . . and out in a light long curve, see . . . ?

Annemarie Perhaps there'll soon be another mite now. . .

Nora But knitting . . . it's always so unsightly. Anyway, capitalism is male domination carried to extremes, I'm sick of it.

Throwing the knitting in a corner, **Annemarie** *runs after it, kneels on the floor and carefully picks up the fallen stitches again.*

Annemarie That was a present for Ivan! A new pullover for his birthday.

Nora When women talk about our periods or children it's our ability to reproduce that comforts us. Our only certainty is how much we have to endure.

Annemarie Once I've got the knitting back to rights, I'll wrap up Emmy's beautiful walky talky doll. There's the door.

Nora Well, hurry up!

Annemarie *gets up with a groan to open the door.* **Weygang** *sticks his head in, pretending to be bashful, then comes to* **Nora** *with a bunch of flowers.*

Weygang I've come for a heart-to-heart with this angry little woman. As we talk things over I'll enjoy watching this angry little woman. Anger can add to a woman's beauty. It makes her blaze.

Annemarie I'll slip away as the man and woman want to be on their own.

She goes.

Nora Things often click between men and women when they're on their own. As they say: it just clicked.

Weygang You've still got the tarantella in your blood, I see. And it makes you even more of a temptress. Whooch! Your eyes are flashing, your cheeks gleaming with excitement, your teeth sparkling with anger!

Nora First one must cause the collapse of the family, then cause everything else to collapse.

Weygang Your hair and breath are quivering! And your chest is quivering as you breathe.

Nora *runs headfirst into his belly. Laughing, he holds her tight, they wrestle,* **Weygang** *does not take it seriously, smiling he wards her off.*

Weygang You're trembling, whatever's getting at you . . .

Annemarie (*looking in at the door, shocked*) That's not the proper environment if the children are to grow up proper.

11

At **Helmer**'*s.* **Mrs Linde** *flutters round* **Helmer**, *eager and intrusive.*

Linde Torvald honey, tea's just ready! Isn't that marvellous? Your ex-wife, Nora, would never have known how to make tea like this.

Helmer *is silent.*

Linde Darling! One lump of sugar, two lumps of sugar or three lumps of sugar?

Helmer Four lumps.

Linde But you've never taken four lumps of sugar?! And the table is laid. Isn't that splendid?

Helmer *is silent.*

Linde What seem like trivial actions, say putting sugar in tea, make me so happy. You haven't any idea!

Helmer They leave me stone cold.

Linde Because every time they make me think how my best energies and abilities have been a waste of effort.

Helmer Wasted?

Linde Helmer honey – at office-work of course! I'm far too creative to endure office-work – through your help I've realised that, honey! Your ex, Nora, never did. Easing children's first steps in life is creative, isn't it? Especially deeply disturbed children who've been left by their mother, their real mother?

Helmer Yes well . . .

Linde These things are beyond men. That's why we love you – there's always some mystery between a man and a woman.

Helmer Certain people, such as gushing women, aren't let in too close.

Linde Once bitten, twice shy, Torvald. Believe me, Nora wasn't worth it! These patient woman's hands of mine will soon change all that. Women can do one thing well: wait, even if for years.

Helmer Now Nora's left me, I must be alone a lot to listen to my heart. What it says will decide my future. I've got the rough outline already: my heart says high finance.

Linde Love-songs don't last for ever after.

Helmer I've been so badly wounded I don't like anyone too close.

Linde Only a man can talk like that! So proud, so hard-hearted.

Helmer I've become a lone wolf, always hunting alone – which is why women go for me.

Linde Other women mustn't go for you! You're only to open your whole heart to me, Torvald!

Helmer Well, what about Krogstad?

Linde Krogstad – nothing doing there.

Helmer But why not?

Linde Krogstad doesn't radiate power – and I'm so addicted to it. It just radiates out of you. Krogstad has no standing in the business world. You're the best catch for me!

Helmer I'm the best catch for women who could do better than you!

Linde Trying to make your little Linde a bit jealous? It's not fair, tormenting an inferior you really love.

Helmer Why don't you get hold of someone deeply inferior, like Krogstad, someone on your own level?

Linde Can you smell my home-made biscuits, dearest Torvald? I baked them specially for you.

Helmer I've no time for such things, as you know.

Absent-mindedly, he stuffs his face with biscuits.

Linde Have a smell, Helmer, do just once, just for me!

Helmer Can't you see I'm tied up in the financial news?

Linde Talking of being tied up, Torvald . . .

Helmer Yes?

Linde Shall we play our game, our game for long nights?

Helmer What do you mean?

Linde A hard man who's always busy hunting, turns all and sundry into fair game once he closes his bedroom door! That's the natural balance.

Helmer Ooh my little Linde . . .

Linde We've risen above petty moral constraints, haven't we, Torvald? And I never tell a soul about it.

Helmer Do you want . . . right now . . . ?

Linde To be your mistress, right, Torvald!

With some effort she puts on her boots.

Helmer I've no time right now . . . I really . . . the financial news . . .

Linde Oh yes you do, Torvald! Come on! Come here!

Helmer As long as you tell no one about it.

Linde No one! It's our special secret, Torvald.

Pulling him.

Helmer But the children might come back at any moment . . .

Linde Long before the children get back we'll be worn out by the whip. They went to the pond to feed the swans.

Helmer Well get on then!

Outside door. Children's voices.

Linde Damn it! Oh . . . my instincts immediately tell me to rush and hug the children. Their walk must have been cut short by the weather. Your poor little ones with no mother!

Hurrying out. From outside:

You look so bright and cheerful! My, what red cheeks you've got. Like apples and roses.

Children's voices throughout.

Did you have fun? That's marvellous. Yes; you pulled Emmy and Bob on the sledge? Both of them? You're such a smart boy, Ivan. Ooh, my sweet little baby doll! What? You pelted each other with snowballs? Oh, if only I'd been with you! . . .

12

Weygang'*s office.* **Weygang** *and* **Helmer**. *Both busy brandishing cognac and cigars. 'Masculine' atmosphere.* **Helmer** *emanates servility.*

Weygang (*quietly aside*) So here we have the weak link in person. (*Aloud to* **Helmer**.) You must know, old boy, what brings us together: capital.

Helmer Thank you, Consul. You've put it just right, capital rubs off both of us as I keep telling my housekeeper, Mrs Linde. In my job I aim to honour my commitments to capital at all times.

Weygang Splendid, Helmer. Have you only recently joined our club?

Helmer I've only just had the honour, Consul. But I'm already darting round like a shark, sorry, a pike toing and froing between the er, petrified pillars of high finance – letting in fresh air, Consul.

Weygang No need to call me Consul! I hope you don't think of me as a petrified pillar?!

Helmer I'd never do such a thing, Mr Weygang, Sir.

Weygang Well, we can always use fresh blood. If I'm rightly informed, you're currently an executive at the Accounts Bank, eh Helmer?

Helmer But I'm all out for change, for the sound of my coffers filling up, Consul.

Weygang Do let's drop business for once, Helmer!

Helmer I can't, Consul Weygang – it's part of my flesh and blood. I was born to speculate with facts and figures, Consul!

Weygang You're one of the Stock Market's dazzling prodigies, Helmer.

Helmer I believe so too, Consul. But take a capitalist's children away and you take all his motives for accumulating property and giving employment to people. He'll soon blow the lot!

Weygang I know, I know, Helmer.

Helmer I've got one foot in the market economy, Consul.

Weygang And the other's to follow suit as soon as possible, eh?

Helmer Oh, that'd be wonderful, wonderful, Consul.

Weygang Take your feet out of the market economy and the bank for a moment . . .

Helmer Very hard for me, Consul, I'm so deeply rooted there.

Weygang Span this gap and remember that even a manager of genius must take a rest from managing once in a while . . .

Helmer I've often told Mrs Linde, my housekeeper, I should have made more of myself, Consul . . .

Weygang You must move in the right circles . . .

Helmer Where are these circles, where are these circles, Consul?

Weygang If you're really up to it, I could introduce you to a lady . . .

Helmer Oh, my dear Consul, Sir . . .

Weygang I am not your dear Consul.

Helmer Please forgive me, Consul, I didn't say 'my dear'!

Weygang The lady I refer to fills her hours fluttering from flower to flower.

Helmer Saliva's dripping from my mouth at the mere thought, Consul.

Weygang She's a brand new type of female, what they call 'flappers' in the States.

Helmer I could brush up my English, Consul . . .

Weygang The lady's a creature beyond all moral constraints, but at the same time she looks like a child. Ah . . . (*Significantly.*) and she can frequently be very cruel . . .

Helmer My God . . . the lady's American, you say . . . Consul? Will I even get across to her . . . should one . . . secret wishes . . . a foreigner . . .

Weygang Don't talk rubbish, Helmer! I'll introduce you.

Helmer Oh many many thanks for your generosity. My kind regards to the lady, er . . . won't fail to appear punctually . . .

Weygang I hope so. Punctuality is the politeness of princes, Helmer my man!

13

Nora*'s bedroom.* **Nora** *and* **Annemarie.** **Nora** *in a dressing gown making herself up in front of a mirror.* **Annemarie** *tidying up.*

Annemarie I can't look at it . . . It must hurt the men something awful!

Nora They want it to hurt, Annemarie!

Annemarie I remember my father's horrid floggings when I was a child . . .

Nora Your father was poor and corrupt, Annemarie, these men are naturally rich.

Annemarie High-up men let themselves be beaten . . . Why didn't you beat your children, Nora, if you had to beat anyone? That's a woman's nature.

Nora I'd never beat my children!

Annemarie Making new life's our duty, not destroying old life . . .

Nora It may be yours, it's not mine.

Bell rings.

See who's outside. Can't be him, it's too early.

Annemarie Educated people are never punctual to the second.

Goes to open the door. From outside **Helmer**'s *voice.*

Helmer Punctual to the second! As things stand the slightest detail could make or break my career . . . . Aren't you . . . . Aren't you . . .

Annemarie Annemarie. My goodness, Mr Helmer!

Their voices become more distinct, a bit later **Annemarie** *bursts in through the door.*

Madam Nora, Nora! It's Mr Helmer! It's your Mr Helmer! Are the married couple getting back together again at long last?!

Nora I know who it is, Annemarie.

Takes her dressing gown off. Underneath she's wearing sado-gear, high leather boots etc. Holding a riding-whip she puts on a mask.

Annemarie He must've come to talk about the children. Show some common sense, my little Nora.

Tries to take away her whip and mask. **Nora** *pushes her away.*

What God has joined together let no man put asunder. Nora! Be sensible!

Nora *pushes* **Annemarie** *away so fiercely she stumbles, almost falling.*

My Nora always does what's right. If a mother remembers her children, instinct makes her do what's right. If I'd kept my child, I wouldn't have done many of the wrongs in my life.

Nora Shut your trap, Annemarie! Don't tell him who I am!

Annemarie I'd never shove myself between man and wife – it's easier to destroy what connects them than a spider's web.

Goes out. After a while **Helmer** *comes in awkwardly.* **Nora** *stands motionless.*

Helmer Oh good evening, gentle madame, I trust I find you . . . oh . . . come here, it's so hard going through life without a helpmate, one's so helpless . . .

Bowing, he presents her with a bunch of flowers.

May I be permitted . . .

Nora *throws them in a corner.*

My dear lady, already started? . . . I'm just coming! . . . do say to me: there, slave, now I've made you into a nice tight, stiff, sadistic, tied-up, tied-together parcel to help your circulation . . .

Trying out the furniture with a finger.

You've a lovely home! Lovely furniture, real taste. Of course I'd prefer dark Caucasian walnut to pale oak, but still . . . top quality . . . er, our sense of taste derives from the human as an individual. Human beings can only preserve individuality in a free market economy.

Nora Please kneel down!

Helmer Excuse me, gentle madame. But you seem familiar to me somehow, your figure I mean.

Wants to touch her, but then his nerve fails him.

You look like someone. Shouldn't we roll back the carpet first? Er . . . I wouldn't like to soil it unnecessarily . . . then I'll ask you to gag me so foxily, bind my face so tightly with one of your petticoats I can't get it off on my own, and once I surrender to you, drop all my defences, I'll even ask you to make fun of me, say vicious, vulgar things to me . . .

Nora On your knees!

Helmer Sorry. At once.

Awkwardly lifts his trouser legs and kneels down.

Be so kind as to ensure no one can eavesdrop. To reassure me. The lady, I mean that old slut of a skivvy, I know her . . . you too . . . and please stuff your old silk stockings so tight in my mouth it's only just OK, gag me so cruelly I can't get a sound out . . .

Nora You're an industrialist, I'm told . . . so you must have inside info on the ins and outs of industry . . . ?

Helmer Thank you gentle madame for shackling me! Please put on such skintight, sensual, provocative clothes as only you can, put a skintight black teddy on, so tight it clings and stretches over your sensual, perverse, sumptuous, beautiful, firm, plump, wonderful breasts – so they can't go any higher . . . you slut . . . And I beg you for lovely, dark, long silk stockings and the most becoming shoes you have . . . in future I'll write what I want for you so I get . . .

Nora No, no, not such scared dove's eyes! I forgive your anxiety, but it does insult me. I forgive this insult as further proof of your vast love for me.

Tying him up.

Helmer Business doesn't depend on natural forces with inevitable results but on efficient people doing their jobs.

He is increasingly tied up.

Is it Sèvres, that cup with flowers on . . . ? A home of real style and taste.

Nora I don't want to hear about business in general but about one particular business.

Tying up.

Helmer No man is an island. Big bulk purchasing power ensures profit.

She lashes him.

Not so hard, please.

Nora Longwinded – I want real grit.

Nora *stops lashing.*

Helmer . . . Please, please go on, sweet dear gentle madame . . . Could you please, next time I come, bind me, tie me up into a parcel, wrap me in a pvc apron done up tight, fastened together, with your all-in-one undies tied round my face, so tight I can't get them off and leave me, don't come back till the next day, the day after . . . please leave me shut up in the flat . . . aaah . . .

Nora (*stops lashing and sits down*) I want the goods!

Helmer I'll tell you! I will tell you! (*Groans.*) Next time please soak some rope and leather straps in water first . . .

Nora I'll stop again!

Helmer Oh no, my dearest, my sweetest . . . (*Is lashed, groans.*) According to my information the site and the textile factory have gone down the chute, financially you could say smashed. We plan to close the works because they're unprofitable . . .

Nora And where are these works?

Helmer The meadow-lark, the meadow-lark by daylight doesn't just look dark. Didn't I tell you – please don't lash me so lightly!

Nora (*lashing more hesitantly*) What? Meadow-lark?

Helmer As a general rule there'd be no one left in the dark to palm the site off on. But I did it by starting a rumour about a railway line being built there . . . More, please! (*Is lashed, groans.*) One reason for unprofitability: transport. I'm even more convinced we know each other, gentle madame.

Nora The meadow-lark is to be sold. (*Lashes.*) I'd play squirrel and hop from branch to branch for you. (*Lashes even more wildly.*)

Helmer Stop! Stop, please. That's too much!

In what follows **Nora** *lashes harder and harder.*

Helmer You're right not to stop as soon as I say 'stop' . . . (*Groans.*) and beside that, please, I'd like – put silk stockings on me and tie my stockinged thighs with ropes from top to bottom as tight as only you can . . . (*Groans.*) and then another thing please, that I can't say out loud, I'll write it down till next time . . . (*Groans.*) please rape me rotten, till I pass out . . . all the hours you can spare, take me with my face under your sensuous, perversely pretty behind and bosom – my head between your tightly stockinged thighs . . . (*Groans.*) I'm sure we know each other, gentle madame.

Nora (*lashes*) . . . I'm being so irrational today! The things that get passed down from papa to little daughter! (*Lashes fiercely.*)

Helmer (*groans*) I'll write down more, how you are to, please . . . (*Groans.*) no, I can't say it out loud, I'll write that down too. If total chaos isn't to wipe out economic returns, rules are . . . with no prospect of profit, it must come to a standstill . . .

Helmer *falls over and remains motionless.*

Nora No need to strain my eyes or my delicate little hands any more. (*Takes the mask off.*) Torvald! This is your little bird speaking.

Helmer (*coming slowly to*) Nora!

Nora This year we've no need to be stingy. You'll sell the lark now . . . If your indiscretion doesn't run away with you! If you don't have to take out a loan!

Helmer My God, Nora . . . there's nothing unethical about my plans. They've just revamped their housing estate with loving care . . . you can't think that of me.

Nora Right.

Helmer I admit it with a heavy heart: I lied, Nora!

Nora Is it my squirrel pottering about?

Helmer At least I don't tell Mr Weygang that, although of course it doesn't make any odds!

Nora Or is it my bird twittering about?

Helmer Anyway I'm ruined, if they find out what my ex-wife has become . . . you're destroying a budding relationship by this, Nora! With a young creature.

Nora All the better.

Helmer Nora, for the sake of our children . . . I beseech you . . . don't say a word to anyone . . . no, please, I'm begging you, you who wronged me . . . you left me, abandoned me . . .

Nora Urgh pooh, don't talk such rot!

Helmer For the sake of our former love . . .

Nora Pooh, don't say such drivel! You've still got the tarantella in your blood, I see. Makes you even more of a temptress.

Pause. **Nora** *sits on the bed breathing heavily. After a while she pulls the bell.* **Annemarie** *comes, unties the bound and moaning* **Helmer**, *helps him onto his legs, brushes his suit and leads him out.*

Annemarie (*coming back*) That wasn't very nice of my little Nora – to think I rocked you in my arms. Poor man! And his suit was proper filthy, it'll have to be cleaned. Shame on you!

14

Helmer'*s living room.* **Helmer** *and* **Krogstad** *at table.* **Linde** *serving the men.*

Helmer In the time ahead I won't have time for personal happiness.

Linde Oh darling there mustn't be any limits to your personal and professional happiness or you'll do yourself down.

Helmer Well, isn't the meal ready yet?

Linde There are no limits to my devotion for you. My devotion to you is limitless.

Helmer Didn't you hear?

Linde *goes off.*

Linde (*from the kitchen*) Really? Ever such a big dog, running behind you? He didn't bite, did he? No, dogs don't bite good children. Really? Are we going to play? What shall we play then? Hide and seek? Right, let's play hide and seek. Bob's going to hide first. Me? Right, I'll hide first.

Noise from the kitchen, crashing, shattering.

Helmer Tell me, Krogstad . . . we all know from the theatre, you used to love that woman who's now in my kitchen.

Krogstad I've buried that feeling. In future, I won't ever feel anything, as I've recently decided to become a businessman – just like you, Mr Helmer.

Helmer I'd be happy to pass Linde on. You may not know, I'm getting married. A young lady from the cream of society.

Krogstad I've decided to become a businessman but I've got no business.

Helmer Take Linde off my hands and you'll get your business and a reliable assistant.

Krogstad You think she'll swallow that?

Helmer Ah, we men, you and I, we know women . . .

Krogstad I know more of life.

Helmer I know life much better! Listen, you used to be on friendly terms with Nora . . .

Krogstad Yes.

Helmer I've seen her again. In what were for her unspeakably humiliating circumstances, spare me from going into details!

Krogstad Seeing her again must be specially tragic.

Helmer But what's worst is she could ruin everything: my children, my household, me, my reputation, you, Krogstad, Mrs Linde, my future, my business, my situation, my social position, my future marriage . . .

Krogstad (*breaking in*) I'm sure she couldn't smash all that.

Helmer You can't be sure. She's incredibly genned up on business all of a sudden. She didn't get that from me.

Krogstad (*attentive*) What do you mean?

Helmer She could drive me to the abyss – even right into it!

Krogstad Then she's got some power.

Helmer (*furious*) Course not, not a trace. But I do think about her going on a longish journey abroad . . .

Krogstad . . . or not existing any more . . .

Helmer Don't say such things! Better to show you're ambitious, greedy for success, greedy for profit, grasping for promotion, you keep your word and honour contracts, Krogstad!

Linde (*coming in with a tray*) Ready! (*To* **Krogstad**.) Isn't it like a knife cutting you up, seeing the deep bonds binding Torvald and me?

Krogstad No pulses, I hope, I'm not to eat pulses.

Linde (*furious*) If there's anyone who's not to eat something, it's my Torvald! (*She snuggles up to* **Helmer**, *who peevishly rebuffs her. To* **Krogstad**:) As you see, he never thinks of himself, only of me and my reputation . . . we're not really married yet . . . A man can have such tender feelings but look so hard!

She hands out the meal.

Krogstad . . . And sugar peas . . . perfect.

He is about to take some.

Linde (*holding him back*) Let my Torvald have his first. Fingers off!

Helmer Do hold your trap, Linde!

Linde (*to* **Krogstad**) He's only saying that to hide the soft centre he shows when we're on our own.

Helmer Christ, Linde . . .

Linde (*to* **Krogstad**) Could you believe this noble sensitive man sometimes has a mistress, i.e. me?

Krogstad (*looking into another pot*) New potatoes . . . I love them.

15

Factory floor as before. **Eva** *with* **Women Workers** *at their breakfast break. The* **Foreman** *there too, a bit apart.* **Nora** *is visiting, her clothes may be expensive but her whole presence is nonchalant. Bits of fixtures lie about, making it look rather like a D-I-Y shop.*

Worker As you see there have been grand improvements, not least the little works library we've been allowed to set up.

Eva Up till now, you have had to stand with a book at a lighted shop window if you wanted to read. You'll be able to stand outside soon – just wait and see!

Worker Some things are better left unheard, Nora!

Nora Education is being sensitive to beauty, it has to be worked at.

Eva Beauty's here alright. Thank heavens!

Nora Education is being sensitive to culture, it has to be worked at – like character.

Eva But first you need to wipe out poverty and find the time to think. You'll soon have plenty of poverty and time galore for thought. But it'll be too late then.

Worker Don't listen to her, Nora, women who aren't loved can get very tetchy.

Worker The head of Personnel has given us express permission . . .

Worker . . . to found a day nursery for the factory's children.

Worker To keep our minds off the rumours of closure.

Worker But it can hardly be more closed . . .

Worker . . . because social democracy's against it, we're sure of that.

Eva Nice of social democracy to tell you that. If only it supplied better building materials as well.

Foreman Ah, this old bricky says it will last for ever!

Eva *kicks a mounted bookshelf, which falls as the wall gives way.*

Eva It's a pity for ever won't last long here.

Worker (*moaning*) Now you've done it!

Worker Social democracy's taught us to talk to all sorts of people.

Worker You can learn about other people and countries from books.

Eva (*furious*) Just so you don't care about what's happening right in front of you!

Worker At the big right-to-vote demonstration in 1905, I remember your district sending a large troop of women to the procession.

Worker Those women left hearth, home and children to demonstrate for the men's right to vote.

Worker They'll never forget the solemn march past Parliament.

Worker That vast crowd was quiet as a mouse, heads bared.

Worker Not a sound but the firm, sure step of the battalion of workers.

Worker Mobilising the disinherited wasn't for nothing.

Worker . . . only the poorest, the women, are still politically fettered.

Eva Now you've thrown away your fetters – and got your own day nursery! Bravo!

Worker Why knock major social achievements, Eva?

Eva (*screams*) Don't you see why they're tarting it all up now – now of all times? After it's all fallen to bits here?

Worker They're feeling remorse and want to make some amends.

Worker They're ashamed of being uncharitable before.

Eva Our Berlin colleagues carry 31 comrades to their graves. They stand up for their right to a peaceful Mayday demonstration and get provoked! They die from the bullets of SPD Chief Constable Zörgiebel and his coppers!

Worker My God, Eva, that's over and done with! Social democracy has now seen the light.

Nora (*who has been stiff and distant, suddenly, rather mannered*) I'm a woman! Women's history to the present day has been the history of our murder. How do we make up for murder without doing fresh violence!

Worker What are you on about?

Nora Everything here will be ripped up, sold – actually it's sold already, not yet ripped up.

Foreman Social democracy guarantees nothing can happen over our heads.

Eva Unless our heads roll.

Worker Those were the bad old days, only another war . . . but that can't happen.

Nora You'll be told your flats must make way for a railway, you'll do very nicely out of it when you use it to go on holiday!

Eva You'll enjoy endless holidays when there's no work, when jobs are shed.

Nora But something far more dangerous is to be built here which will blow your babies' high-chairs sky-high. They do it because you're women – because of this sordid huge hatred of women, they sense women's strength and can't do a thing about it.

Worker I don't understand, Nora.

Nora Men sense women's huge inner power. In blind fear they wipe women out.

Foreman You're talking in riddles, Nora. This fanaticism is making you almost ugly!

Worker Yes, I don't think she's as beautiful as she was.

Nora It's another kind of beauty, inside. It's not as fashionable as the outer kind.

Worker I'd settle for beauty outside that everyone can see.

Nora Nothing's worse than being a sexual parasite. I won't be one a moment longer.

Eva The floor we stand on will be ripped up!

Nora Women don't belong to themselves. From now on I belong to me.

Worker That's why you're ugly – you're not part of the great whole.

Worker We're all part of this greatness and this whole. We all fit.

Worker . . . it's this harmony that gives us beauty.

Nora Listening to you I feel like putting a match to the lot!

Worker You're crazy, Nora.

Worker And deformed, Nora.

Worker And dehumanised, Nora.

Worker (*shaking her head*) Put a match to what set us free – the machine?

Nora 'Serving a machine, a woman forfeits her femininity, while she castrates and humiliates her husband by taking the bread out of his mouth.' Mussolini.

Worker We've no fascists here!

Eva They take the machine from you. Women are hit hardest because we've been at it less long.

Nora It takes your freedom so burn it! If your husbands get burnt too, so what, they sent you to the machine and use it to double and treble your load, but they give nothing in return.

Worker Anarchy! Terrorism!

Nora Women are beheaded, cut to pieces. They're allowed to keep their bodies but their heads must be knocked off as that's where thinking goes on.

Worker But without a body . . .

Nora . . . for him to walk over . . .

Worker . . . a husband gets nothing!

Worker We know our husbands, they've got nothing anyway . . .

Worker . . . can't deprive us of ourselves.

Nora Your husbands've got you, you've got nothing!

Worker Wrong, it goes both ways.

Worker Still we've got the children.

Nora Your husband doesn't want them, he gives them a wide berth.

Foreman Men are turned off by this, Nora. Women might not be so much, but then women aren't really concerned.

Worker Of course women are turned off by it too.

Worker Well, I don't find Nora pleasing.

Worker Nor me!

Nora As she can't please women any more, she takes the first stride towards liberation. One step against the base of a pyramid of silent power . . .

Eva (*has for some time been silent, she suddenly begins to scream, gets worked up into hysterics, and has to be held tight*) I'm a woman too. I'm a woman like Nora! I hop about with little screams of delight, whirl about, till you can hardly see me for dust, drape myself round the neck of the first man I see, grab every chance for a kiss, slide across the floor like a boisterous little girl, just catching myself in time, throw my arms in glee round any dear man, shower him with thanks for a piece of chocolate, walk on my hands, brace myself, laughing loudly when I pull it off, my feet above my chosen man's face, I play: *Let the robbers march in, across the golden bridge*, I name the robbers in order of appearance: Deutsche Bank plc, Berlin Bank plc, Dresden Bank plc, Bank of Commerce and Industry plc, Bank of Public Economy plc, Mortgages and Discount Bank plc, National Bank and Giro Institution, Club Bank, Berlin Bank of Commerce plc, Hard Slomann Bank Co. Ltd, Marquand and Co's Banking House, Max Merck et Cie, Accounts Bank plc, Simon's Bank plc, H.J. Stein, Warburg, Brinkmann, Wirtz and Co . . .

The **Workers** *bend over her, cover her and speak pityingly to her, the* **Foreman** *remains aside, smoking a cigarette,* **Nora** *sits there motionless. Pause.*

Nora I could tear the fancy-dress costume into a hundred thousand pieces.

16

Weygang *comes in wearing tennis whites with* **Nora** *draped round his neck.*

Nora Fate says we're made for each other. You don't just drop relationships once they get tough.

Weygang I don't agree.

Nora I'm certain there's still something between us. But you must help me towards a new start.

Weygang I'm certain the ageing process and death are ahead of you. First the change of life. Your sexual organs will decompose on you then. That's not something I'd like to experience.

Nora Wrong! Fate says the opposite. It whispers that we belong together for ever.

Weygang Stop pushing your luck! Besides your thighs and upper arms are orange-peely and that always scares women.

Nora There's nothing wrong with my skin. A man in love sees behind the shell, to the woman's feelings.

Weygang Squeeze the skin on your thighs and there's your death sentence: little dents!

Weygang *keeps casually, lightly fiddling with this and that.*

Nora The meadow-lark's why you're addicted to me. A large-scale industrial project is under way and you know why. Thinly populated, cooling water galore. The site's value will rise astronomically. We both belong to you, the land and I.

Weygang All long past their sell-by date, my dearest.

Nora (*not listening to him anyway*) I've not breathed a word about it. I only open my whole heart to you.

Weygang Transaction already signed, sealed and delivered. As always, Nora in the dark, Helmer bankrupt, Helmer dishonourably fired by the bank, board meeting. Game, set and match: Weygang.

Nora (*still not listening as she whisks impishly about with a little toy feather duster*) A person with no pride would call it blackmail.

Weygang If you keep quiet, I'll set you up in a little fabric or stationery shop – whichever you prefer – being a woman, probably fabrics.

Nora I'll blackmail you through the union, the press, if need be the Accounts Bank board of trustees.

Weygang What for?

Nora I'm only doing it for your own good.

Weygang I said I've already bought the property in question. Helmer's a halfwit.

Nora (*still not listening*) Blackmail, blackmail, see! (*Unbearably impish and childish.*) I'm feeling playful so I'll do my favourite gymnastics again to show you how elastic I am.

Crossing to the climbing bars, she's held tight by **Weygang**.

Weygang (*earnestly*) Climbing the bars will display your drooping bum and boobs. So don't do it! Which would you rather, fabric or stationery?

Nora (*puzzled, as it slowly dawns on her*) Which would I?

Weygang Fabric or paper?

Nora (*stricken*) I'd rather stay with you . . .

Weygang You can't, you have to stay at your place. That's why I wouldn't like to be in your shoes. Especially now you're past your sell-by date.

Nora *stands there numb.*

17

On the bars hang stockings and sexy underwear. **Nora** *wears a frilly pink tutu with spotted plush top. She is garishly made up. A man goes out, getting dressed. The* **Minister** *sits on the big pink satin bed taking his clothes off. Brothel atmosphere.*

Minister You've not come up with any new ideas, for some time my dear. You've done no gymnastics on the apparatus for ages – that's my special treat as there's always a chance you'll split in two and fall to the floor. Nothing like enough action here.

Nora I'm disgusted with this life.

Minister Trying to say I disgust you? I can tell you a woman who sells herself is always more disgusting than the man who buys.

Nora I mustn't do it a second longer than I want.

Minister Talk like that from a woman like you is an appeal for a man to take her away.

Nora I can have my own business at any time. Whenever I want.

Minister Congratulations!

Nora (*snuggling up to him*) Do I seem like a squirrel or a little roe deer, Minister?

Minister A roe deer – you don't leave the ground any more. I'll only pay the basic rate for what you offer, as you'll appreciate.

Nora Consul Weygang was about to kill himself for me. He saw no other way out of his passion.

Minister I'd kill myself too if you were constantly around.

Nora It's up to me at any time when I want the business.

Minister Is Weygang paying?

Nora Yes. To punish himself. He doesn't know he could come back at any time. We're each waiting for the other to make the first move.

Krogstad *comes in shooting a water pistol.*

Krogstad Look, Mrs Helmer, this could just as easily have been a real pistol.

Nora It couldn't. The security guard would have stopped you.

Krogstad No security guard in sight. As I can see, you're just dealing with problems of love. I myself spend more time on financial transactions. Your ex-husband, Helmer, wants me to kill you because you're in the way of his advancement.

Nora You what? Get out!

Minister You're a bit late. Don't you know Helmer's ruined!

Krogstad Whaat? I've been ill or I'd have got here before today to commit this murder.

Nora Let me list this man's honorary posts – he's in a different class: Honorary Consul of a Latin American state, international arms dealer, President of one of the biggest chambers of industry and commerce, President of the Wholesalers and Exporters Association, Director of the Economic Consortium of the Chemical Industry, and of the Employers' Consortium in the regional association.

Krogstad (*breaking in*) As I see it you're obviously a victim of compulsory and systematic redundancies.

Minister Don't let your clients see each other so indiscreetly, my dear Nora. Or I won't add a tip.

Krogstad Are you the minister I know from the *Daily Messenger*? Indulging greed creates new hungers, which proves that governments actively handing out care to their citizens only provoke individual discontent about too little cash or goods.

Minister (*to* **Nora**) So now you receive reps. That's the beginning of the end at least as far I'm concerned.

Krogstad I'm not a rep, though it was capital that sent me. May I take this occasion to beg your protection, Minister. In any case I've seen you too long in this compromising situation.

Minister It's obvious you're not in capital. Refer the matter to my personal manager.

Nora (*screaming*) Once I get my new business, I'll never see you shits again! Piss off both of you and take your cocks with you or I'll throw them out after you.

Minister Don't worry, I'd never dream of leaving a woman like you here.

Krogstad Right now I'm holding my own purse out. May I mention your name, Minister? You won't forget?

Minister I'm going, it's so fidgety here. I miss the feminine ambience. And it's unclean.

Nora (*calling after them as they go out*) Why should the Minister, my protector, give you money?

Krogstad *starts to speak, but then makes a disparaging gesture, and, as* **Nora** *doesn't twig, taps his forehead and vanishes.*

Nora (*shouting*) Let the public purse give you money!

Krogstad (*half outside*) The public purse takes, it doesn't ever give. Takes from creative entrepreneurs.

Minister (*from outside*) He won't satisfy her the way I do!

Nora *thinks briefly. Then tries to pull herself up the bars, she manages, but only with an effort, and falls back down with a quiet sound of pain.*

18

In **Helmer**'*s dining room.* **Helmer** *sits at supper reading a newspaper,* Idyll. **Nora** *serving him.*

Helmer (*taking a drink of tea*) Only three lumps of sugar again, not four lumps! Can't you be more careful?

Nora Prize bleater. You left me frustrated again last night.

Helmer Only the middle class have a problem with orgasms, so I read – proles don't ever have them.

Nora Well thank heavens I'm middle-class, not a prole.

Helmer Was that lover who dumped you better than me?

Nora He didn't dump me, how often must I keep telling you?

Helmer Do you know what we saved last month? That's the way capital begins, Nora!

Nora Have you cast an eye over the new spring samples, Torvald? The designs are gorgeous for the ladies' fabrics. Mandels in Central Square haven't had a range as wide as this for ages . . .

Helmer These Jews are beginning to get too big for their boots! I've still got to repair the loo window later on.

Nora Ah Torvald, surely we can get someone in for that . . .

Helmer Out of the question. At this stage of building up capital nothing must be withdrawn.

Pause, he leafs solemnly through the paper.

Do you know that as I heard of my ruin my icy hands felt the pistols my father left me . . . Doesn't that still make you shake and shiver through your whole body?

Nora You say that three times a day!

Helmer (*furious*) No dessert? You're unkind, Nora. When dessert gives me such pleasure! Now straight after the roast I've got to listen to the business news, you know that doesn't agree with me!

Children's voices behind the door, **Nora** *rushes across, tears open the door and screams.*

Nora Hold your mouths, you bloody brats! Your father wants the business news!

Children quiet. **Helmer** *turns the radio on.*

Radio Announcer . . . we've just heard the well-known textile works PAF (Payer Fibres), named after the synthetics pioneer, Alfred Payer, burnt down in the night of Saturday/ Sunday. Details of the works' recent change of hands will be given on the business news . . .

Nora Did you hear? The bold man put a match to it! Now he'll even scoop the insurance money, the lot . . . . He's so far-sighted!

Helmer I'm far-sighted too, Nora! What I see in the far distance frightens me so much I'd rather stay nearby in our pretty home . . .

Nora . . . I know, it pulls him to me by invisible threads, I was the most important of all his vast range of relationships with the most beautiful women . . . but he's afraid of facing you again, my husband . . .

Helmer *grins dirtily.*

Nora And now we lie awake at night with feverish eyes, one here, the other there . . . and neither of us can . . .

Helmer (*brutally*) Shut your trap. I want to listen!

Nora *is offended.*

Radio Announcer Now business news, beginning with the bulletins: on March the first the TEXO-group, merged with Rhine Chemicals plc, took over Payer-Fibres (PAF), owned by the Accounts Bank plc . . .

Helmer (*excited*) Now they'll talk about me! Listen! They're talking about me!

Nora Who gives a toss about you!

Radio Announcer . . . which recently had to fight sales resistence. On June the first the new combine Texopa, with a 66 per cent share in textile-subsidiary TORACO, merged with the state-run International Chemical Fibres Research in exchange for a 47 per cent stake in the new company (INTERTEX) and 58 million in cash. As agreed, the Government will subsidise INTERTEX up to a period of 10 years to the tune of about 250 million. To maintain a West Europe market share of around 12 per cent the company is also guaranteed contracts to the order of 900 millions on the part of the state.

Pause.

As you heard in the evening news, fire raged through the night at the old PAF-works. The cause of the fire is not yet known. We've heard no more about the fate of the works or of the workers' housing nearby. Consul Fritz Weygang, whose syndicate owned the plant, is at this stage only offering assurances for the quickest possible reconstruction, to safeguard jobs. Payer-Fibres (PAF) has made itself a good international name through its collaboration with French department stores and by manufacturing exclusive issues.

Helmer (*excited*) Did you hear? Did you hear? Nora?! Talking about me.

Nora *pours him a coffee, from the radio comes a march – echoes of earlier German fascism.*

Nora I must invite the great man once more! Those terrors haven't smashed all the china with flowers on yet.

Helmer He won't come even if you invite him hundreds of times . . .

Nora . . . Because he's shy of you . . .

Helmer I wonder if the Jews put a match to it.

Nora, *offended, goes to the radio to switch off the march.*

Helmer Just leave it, Nora! I love listening to that music!

As the stage darkens slowly, we hear a march. Curtain.

What Happened After Nora Left Her Husband

Jelinek's subtitle – *Pillars of Society* – may remind us of a shady railway deal but her resolution is more pessimistic than Ibsen's. Her businessman does not give up wheeler-dealing after an appeal to his higher self, for no modern hero could be saved by such optimism. When, one black Wednesday, our nation loses £2 billion, it passes unperturbed into history and we cannot call it to justice. Hardly a year passes without a minister being caught with his knickers down and promptly rewarded by vast fees from the media. Powerful figures, their reputations and relationships so often based on a series of lies, how could a modern dramatist offer the spirit of truth or justice as a credible solution? Here a Marxist views a democracy where big corruption is also not investigated. The pillars of society now are so often rotten, it's only a question of time which paper digs for the dirt first.

Just as international speculators help a currency on a downward slide Nora is bought by Weygang when she's going cheap and offloaded later for a better deal. Women here are as much a commodity as a factory, a site or a currency. Whether a Weygang builds a factory or a nuclear power station the means are the same – deliberately pushing down the real value of his own currency and exploiting the weak to gain even more personal wealth. These business practices, sanctioned by government, are seen to lead to the depression that in turn led to the Third Reich and to Helmer's beloved Nazi march. Because Jelinek is more pragmatic, her solution is more pessimistic than both the Ibsen plays, with Nora being defused by becoming part of the capitalist world, corrupted by her dealings, tainted by both Weygang and Helmer. The knowledge that might have empowered her leaves her dispossessed rather than determined, dependent rather than hopeful.

By looking on from the innocence of a former age at a society riddled with untruths, Jelinek's Nora is too shocked to see what we accept – that corruption runs through all relationships. Her earlier naïve belief in Helmer is now shaken by realising that business justifies all. It is hard to understand the commonplaces of capitalism – that businessmen allow themselves special rewards, that women are dispensable once they have served as rungs on the ladder to success. She cannot see through the smoke screen which makes blatant personal advancement look like beneficent service to the community. As our businessmen in the eighties Weygang believes in the licensed greed that gives special moral status to having the cash to be enterprising. This image of power must threaten the position of women – Jelinek coolly presents them in a job-lot as victims of man's aggressive need to possess. We may wonder at Nora's naïvety but historians looking back at the eighties will surely be equally astounded at privatisation's never-never promises of better service in order to strip the masses of what they already owned while giving a few individuals even greater power.

Since *A Doll's House*, the social system of the family may have been smashed in the great social upheavals after two World Wars, but women are still having to be strong enough to take humiliation at home and financial exploitation at uncongenial work and are still vulnerable to the demands of other people's views and needs of them. And, like Ibsen's, this Helmer only sees Nora as his homemaker and sexual playmate. Sex and corruption are so intimately connected with business that Helmer immediately knows the advance Weygang offers will be through the bedroom. Turning the clock back to the 1920s gives the impression that the furore following Nora slamming the door in 1879 resulted in the First World War, just as the time shifts give us a sensation of the interdependence of all that has happened in the last century.

Language is not used to characterise individuals but to bring home the general brutalising of business. Neither the Minister nor the workers are defined by their speech, yet both play games with words and phonemes. For both are equally brutalised by their work, both have ears and mouths distorted by their environment. Jelinek does not flinch from showing the ugliness beneath the pretty veneer of wealth, or of good shop-floor relations in her tough realism. But then Austria came out of the war declaring its citizens as victims of Nazism and has since had a higher growth rate than every other country in the world bar Japan.

Tinch Minter, 1993

Elfriede Jelinek, born in 1946 in Mürzzuschlag, Austria, is one of the most provocative and controversial writers in the German language today. Her novels and plays highlight – from a feminist and socially critical point of view – the failure of manipulated individuals who are prisoners of themselves and of society. Her provocative novels *Die Klavierspielerin* ('The Piano Teacher', 1983) and *Lust* ('Lust', 1989) especially caused a sensation.

Tinch Minter worked as a teacher, theatre administrator and recording manager before becoming a full-time writer. Her many translations with Anthony Vivis range from Botho Strauss's *The Tourist Guide* (Almeida, London), and *The Park* (Sheffield) to Manfred Karge's *The Conquest of the South Pole* which transferred from the Traverse, Edinburgh to the Royal Court, London, before being filmed for Channel 4 and published by Methuen. In 1988 she began her fruitful collaboration with Annie Castledine who directed the first play of Gerlind Reinshagen's war trilogy *Sunday's Children* at Derby. In 1990 she co-translated, with Elisabeth Bond-Pablé, Marieluise Fleisser's *Ingolstadt Plays*. The translations won the first Empty Space award presented by the London Theatre Review and were performed at the Gate Theatre, London and published in *Plays by Women: Nine*. Tinch Minter has recently concentrated on new German women playwrights, Gundi Ellert, Kerstin Specht, as well as other European contemporaries, Edi Shukriu and Lina Wertmüller.

The Choice

Claire Luckham

Characters

The Writer, *a woman in her late forties*
The Consultant, *a man in his fifties or older*
Sal, *a journalist, aged 35*
Ray, *Sal's partner, an illustrator, aged 30*
The Midwife, *in her late thirties*

The Choice received its première at the Salisbury Playhouse on 11 March 1992 with the following cast:

The Writer	Jane Maud
The Consultant	Robert Bathurst
Sal	Toyah Willcox
Ray	David Fielder
The Midwife	Liz Rothschild

Directed by Annie Castledine
Designed by Bill Pinner
Lighting Designer Nick Beadle
Sound Peter Hunter
Deputy Stage Manager Gabrielle Sanders
Video sequence directed by Andrew Reid
Photography by John Greenwood

The Choice was revived by the Theatr Clwyd company at the Emlyn Williams Theatre, Mold on 8 October 1993. The cast was as follows:

The Writer	Noreen Kershaw
The Consultant	Robert Pickavance
Sal	Sally Edwards
Ray	Paul Herzberg
The Midwife	Kim Hicks

Directed by Annie Castledine
Assistant Director Josie Sutcliffe
Designed by Bill Pinner
Lighting Designer Nick Beadle
Company Stage Manager Andrew Gordon
Deputy Stage Manager David Marsland
Assistant Stage Manager Jim Mansell

The play takes place in the present time.
The action takes place continuously in a space that belongs to the writer.

Act One

The **Writer** *enters.*

Writer The Consultant leaves his flat for his office. He notices that the sun is shining, and that there is a slight breeze. His hair is ruffled. It is May. No, not May – March. Better to start earlier in the year. That is because I can't resist thrusting spring – all the burgeoning stuff. New growth, new birth. Start of story. Enough to make you want to throw up.

The **Consultant** *enters.*

Why, oh why, can't he see a little lamb in his mind's eye? (*She sighs.*) The consultant leaves his flat for his office.

Consultant You get used to it, y'know, being God! That's a joke. A mildly depreciative joke. I don't want to be thought arrogant. And in point of fact I go to church. I am a staunch church-goer so . . . you know . . . to think of myself as God would be a sacrilege. However, the fact is, the inescapable fact is, that you have no choice. If people want to stick you up there in the clouds, if they want to create a tin-pot god out of you, then they will. Nothing you can do about it. Goes with the job. Modern expectation of the medical profession is still unbelievably high. Why do I say 'still'? Science can work miracles. They believe in science still, not the church, on matters spiritual. They see me as in control of knowledge and therefore powerful and able to make decisions. In fact I think they want someone around to admire, reverence to the point of allowing that someone to make their decisions for them. And of course, if you make the wrong decision, they can sue you.

Ray *and* **Sal** *enter from opposite sides.* **Sal** *comes in as if from the street.* **Ray** *goes to his desk. He should seem to have been glued to it for the last three hours.* **Ray** *is an illustrator, mostly he illustrates children's books. At the moment he is working on a book about dinosaurs. Reproduction dinosaur bones and drawings litter his side of the stage.*

Sal Hallo!

Ray *is preoccupied.*

Sal Hallo!

Sal *pauses to listen.*

Sal Ray? . . . Working! Goddamn it! Working. Always bloody working!

Ray *stops work.*

Sal I'm pregnant. (*Screams.*) Ray I'm pregnant.

Ray *rushes in.*

Ray Sal, Sal! Darling!

Ray *grabs* **Sal**, *hugging her.*

You are. You really are! That is brilliant! And you are sure?

Sal One hundred per cent certain. As certain as three testing kits and one doctor can make me.

Ray I thought I had something to do with it.

Sal Don't be daft.

Ray Right, I'm daft.

Sal It still doesn't feel real.

Ray Now who is being daft?

Sal Do you think it will when I show?

Ray We must celebrate. What about champagne and bed for starters?

Sal I've got to go to work.

Ray Oh well if you prefer work to hot passionate love.

Sal I'm pregnant.

Ray So why don't we celebrate?

Sal Will it be all right?

Ray What?

Sal I mean if I am pregnant will it be all right?

Ray To celebrate?

Sal It might be bad luck.

Ray Or are you worried about making love?

Sal I don't know. I feel . . .

Ray Are you going to be a miserable stick for nine months?

Sal No. I'm going to be fat and miserable. Fat as a house.

Ray You are going to have a baby. Our kid.

Sal Yes.

Ray I don't believe it.

Sal Don't you?

They look at each other and giggle.

Ray I haven't felt like this . . . since . . . since . . . neanderthal man crawled out of the bog. You know what this means?

Sal Shall we have a cup of tea?

Ray Why not?

Sal I really fancy champers. Why did you mention . . . ?

Ray Do you think it will . . .

Sal Delicious . . .

Ray Damage, affect, hurt the little one?

Sal Her or him? Him or her? Which do you want?

Ray Either either. (*Pronouncing them differently.*) Both.

Sal God help me!

Ray All right, one will do for starters.

Sal Shall we go out and get some bubbly. One glass won't hurt. And then we could come back . . .

Ray One fuck won't hurt the baby.

Sal I should think love will be good for it. And you are loving . . .

Ray I might not be able to. You could say that our love-making has been informed for some time now, informed . . . by trying to make you pregnant. Now that you are . . . I'm not sure that I don't feel slightly redundant. You know I have fulfilled a long and dangerous mission.

Sal Dangerous.

Ray Shouldn't I just curl up and die? Confident that my mission has succeeded, my seed will live on. When I am dead and gone, you can feed off me if you like, suck out my juices and pass them on to the little one.

Sal Christ, Ray!

Ray Do you think we should get married?

Sal Married?

Ray I think this means we should get married. I want to stake out my claim. I want to be sure that I'm around for this baby. Seriously, this is the most important thing that has ever happened to me. Even more important than meeting you. Because I know you and I love you, and this is a commitment to something unknown – and dependent. I want you to be sure and it to be sure, that I am there for it – always. I got champagne. It's in the fridge!

Sal You knew I was pregnant.

Ray You are the one that doubted it.

The Writer The Consultant is in his office. Now . . . I have to start with my brother . . . after all, this is about him. I must put it down and see how it comes out. I don't remember it all by any means – but I do remember some things and I'm sure the more that I think about it, the more other things will come to light, and I'll try to fit them into a pattern, although not necessarily the right pattern. And, of course, you lose things: memories are just memories, and one does lose them, rather they drop away, fall over the precipice and are lost for good. First I remember the seaside and a fancy dress competition. We three went together – dressed as Chinese children. I remember they, everyone, made a great fuss of him. I don't think I was jealous – but the fuss constituted something special, a magic, when we were seen as somehow exotic. Then, I remember being older. These are memories that have to do with him being there, playing outside the gates of the school we went to in the tropics, sitting on an ants' nest. I sat on an ants' nest, I was covered in ants, red ones which bit. I must have screamed like anything. He used to love me being upset like that. There was the time we went to a park where monkeys ran free and you bought peanuts and bananas to feed them with. One rushed up and snatched the banana I was thoughtfully peeling for it out of my hand. I screamed then, and another time I was stung by a jellyfish. I remember howling as the long slimy bits were peeled off my legs leaving rows of little blisters. He used to tell these stories with great gusto, I think is the word, pleasure . . . 'Do you remember? . . . Do you remember? You cried like anything!' I think he must have hated having a younger sister. It was important that I cried. I know he was so often ill, and I wasn't. Nope, I was the perfect baby. And he wasn't.

Ray *is working.* **Sal** *enters, she carries shopping.*

Sal Hallo!

Ray *doesn't respond.* **Sal** *listens to see if he will.*

Sal Working!

Sal *unpacks her shopping. She finds some onions, puts them on the chopping board and starts to cut them up. She begins to feel awful.*

Sal Damn.

She struggles against feeling sick.

Sal Working, always bloody working.

Sal *picks up the chopping board and the onions and throws them on the floor. She looks at them.* **Ray** *comes to watch her.* **Sal** *doesn't see him and shouts.*

Ray! Ray!

Ray What is it, my darling? You've thrown onion all over the place. What's wrong?

Sal I didn't throw . . .

Ray All right.

He starts to pick up the onions.

Sal Not throw . . .

Ray OK.

Sal I don't want to throw up. I don't want to cook.

Ray I'll cook.

Sal Irrational behaviour. That's what it is. Irrational behaviour.

Ray It's OK.

Sal I feel awful.

Ray Don't cry.

Sal (*accusing him*) You are smoking!

Ray I'm sorry.

Sal (*trying not to gag*) Put it out.

Ray OK. How was work?

Sal Oh that! Awful. Smokey. I could hardly stay in the room.

Ray How was the article received?

Sal I don't know. All right. He liked it. I hate editors.

Ray I believe you.

Sal Bastard. Why don't you ever answer me when I come in? I said 'Hallo'. You never answer.

Ray I know.

Sal Oh God, put that fag end out.

Ray It's out.

Sal Right out. Right out of here. It stinks.

Ray Come on little fag end.

Sal I'm sorry, sorry . . . You've no idea. I feel raw inside. You do nothing but work.

Ray Sal!

Sal I want to see you. Now I'm pregnant. I want you to come out from under the piles of bones, the dinosaurs' world. I want you with me, in my world, Ray.

Ray I am in your world, I slept with you Sal. I held your hand. I made you tea in the morning.

Sal I was sick.

Ray I mopped it up. What do you want me to cook?

Sal Vegetables.

Ray And?

Sal Oh!

Ray Are we vegetarian now?

Sal I can't go into a butcher's!

Ray Leave the shopping and cooking to me. I'll do it.

Sal I can't.

Ray Till you feel better.

Sal All that meat hanging up. And the way their hands get ingrained with it. Have you ever noticed a butcher's nails, Ray? They've got blood underneath them like some people have dirt.

Ray And I have ink.

Sal I'm glad we decided not to get married until after the baby is born. Wouldn't it be awful to be sick at your own wedding? Do you Sally Maria take this man to be your lawfully wedded . . . (*Makes throwing up noises.*) I musn't do that I might be sick.

Ray Go to the bathroom.

Sal The clinic is tomorrow. Will you come?

Ray If you want me to.

Sal I want . . . Yes, I want you to sit in the corridor on a hard chair. I shall feel like a little girl at school with her mum waiting, outside.

Ray Thanks.

Sal Ray, I want you there.

Ray I'll be there. I'll bring your milk and gym shoes.

Sal I was never any good at gym!

The **Consultant** *enters.*

Consultant You know what obstetrics is? It's the science of midwifery. In point of fact the unit I'm attached to is run by our midwives. When I came up to take over they told me that. They looked at me to see how I would take it. In some departments the midwives are, well, relegated. A pair of hands, you know the sort of thing. It's not thought they have anything up top so they aren't given responsibility. A unit like that would be run a little like a battery farm. The guy in my job would be enthusiastic about caesarian births. Anything to make giving birth into a mechanical act. I call them advocates of the steel womb. Robot birth.
Mrs Wringer?

Sal *enters.*

Sal Miss or Ms, if you don't mind.

Consultant Not married?

Sal I would have thought that was obvious.

Consultant Sorry. I meant are you going it alone? Are you one of those women who has decided to do without men?

Sal No. My partner is outside.

Ray *enters with sketch pad and chair. He sits and draws.*

Consultant Have you talked about the birth?

Sal Um . . .

Consultant Do you know if he wants to be there? Does he want to be involved?

Sal I think so.

Consultant Do you want him in here now?

Sal Oh.

Consultant It's just a suggestion.

Sal I . . . hadn't thought. Well, it's not important is it? Not this time.

Consultant As you like.

The **Midwife** *enters.*

Consultant Now we are going to take your blood pressure. Then we are going to do a scan, just to see that there is a baby there. That might seem daft, but I always feel happier when I've seen something on the screen. Also, it gives us some idea of how old the foetus is. It's as well to make sure our dates all coincide. Then we're going to take some blood. Now I should tell you about these blood tests. We shall be testing for all the normal things, making sure you've got enough iron in your blood etc. But in addition we would like to offer you the Bart's Test.

Sal What's that?

Consultant I was hoping you were going to ask. Sometimes it's called the triple test. It's optional. You don't have to have it if you don't want. It's three tests that have been developed to measure certain chemicals in your blood. A way of testing for abnormalities on the baby's chromosome structure. The tests won't, of themselves, give us conclusive proof that there is anything wrong, but they will give us an indication.

Sal What happens if there is anything?

Consultant We do other tests. These are just to enable us to pick up on anything at an early stage. As far as I can see there is nothing for you to worry about. Nothing in your notes to give me cause for anxiety. And you're what? Thirty-five? Everything should be fine.

Sal I hope so.

Consultant So we'll do the test, shall we?

Sal Please.

Consultant Good.

Writer The Consultant washed his hands. He wanted it to be lunchtime. He'd seen twelve women that morning and still had three to go. He wanted his lunch and he wanted a rest, and most of all he wanted the afternoon off. He wanted to take his dog for a long walk, and forget about work.

Ray (*as he draws*) Women with swollen bellies. All shapes, all sizes of women, carrying babies. Lumps under their clothes, strange growths, strange foetuses . . . Dear Foetus, how can I help being so jealous? Reply please on a postcard. I'll try to hide it but it gnaws at my insides . . . I'm pregnant with jealousy! Not a man, no. She can have as many men. I don't mean that. I say that because she's got my baby . . . I want to be the one with the baby, in there, seeing the doctor, getting all the attention. The doctors peering at my stomach, sticking their rubbered hands up my vagina. I wouldn't mind being sick. I want to be the mother of a foetus. (*He draws.*) Dear foetus.

Sal *enters.* **Ray** *doesn't notice.*

Sal What are you doing?

Ray Nothing. (*He shuts his pad hurriedly.*) Waiting for you!

Writer I know he was often ill, my brother. He didn't have colds; he had pneumonia. I know this because I was told it. They took him to a clinic in Switzerland. I was left with my Grandfather. I remember picking primulas – all the different colours. I was two and a half when they came back, and they fed him onion and brown sugar, I remember that too. Were they hoping for a miracle? Or did they think just to toughen him up? Mum used to have it as a sort of creed, she wanted to bring him up like any normal child. I never got to eat onion and brown sugar. So he was already different. I found a letter recently written by a doctor when he was six months old, the words 'high grade' are used and 'mongol'. He was born in the war, and when I think of him being stuck in a category it is impossible not to think of Hitler . . . somehow I can't think of what he did with the categories of people that weren't acceptable, that didn't belong . . . I think Mum must have been aware of the awfulness of that thought and cherished him some more.

Sal *comes into the flat.* **Ray** *is at his desk.*

Sal Hallo!

Sal *doesn't wait for an answer.* **Ray** *doesn't answer but listens.* **Sal** *is only interested in finding a loaf of bread and getting herself something to eat. She cuts bread, butters it, puts jam on it.* **Ray** *comes to watch her.*

Ray What are you doing?

Sal Eating.

Ray I can see that.

Sal What do you mean, what am I doing? Isn't a person allowed to eat? I'm making a pig of myself. Have we any bacon?

Ray Yes.

Sal What I really fancy is a bacon butty.

Ray Won't it make you sick?

Sal Sick?

Ray Yeah.

Sal I don't feel sick!

Ray *grins at her.*

I don't. It's gone. I feel wonderful. Ray, Ray. I feel terrific!

Ray Take it easy.

Sal I want to get into this baby now. Planning and . . . can we buy things? Little booties, and fluffy rabbits, teething rings. Ray, teething rings!

Ray They aren't born with teeth.

Sal Richard the Third was. Dear Christ, it is so wonderful to be OK again, not to feel so . . . like an animal looking for a place to crawl in. And not having fears. No more fears that I am giving birth to a three-legged stool or a juggernaut . . .

Ray I've got something to show you.

Sal Oo, Ray, you've bought a matinee jacket.

Ray No, something I've been doing. I didn't want to show you before. Not when you felt . . .

Sal Not something to do with dinosaurs . . .

Ray Come on.

He takes her into his area.

Sal I'm fed up with centrosauruses and triceratops and gigantic footprints . . .

Ray I'm making us a book. I think of it as a kind of diary, a pictorial diary . . . It's the baby since day one. You see I've done quite a bit of research. I decided to draw it as near as possible life-size . . . you know, once it had become big enough. This is what I'm working on now . . . three months . . . You see it is completely formed. I've painted the others in . . . I haven't finished this yet.

Sal Is that how big it is? Really. It's beautiful. Ray. Oh Ray! You're right. I haven't wanted to see any of this. I don't know why not. Oh, but . . . it's so precious. This little thing. You are amazing, you know that. Wonderful.

Ray No, I'm not. I've got a confession to make.

Sal Look at its little fingers!

Ray I'm jealous, Sal, of you having this baby. Please help me.

Sal Darling!

Sal *hugs* **Ray**.

Ray Why can't I have it?

Sal You want to have it?

Ray I want it to be me that's pregnant.

Sal But you're a man.

Ray I know.

Sal I have the babies.

Ray It's not fair!

Sal You can draw. These pictures . . . you know, they've made me feel jealous of it . . . swimming in my foetal waters . . . passing through evolution . . . safe in there. Happy, contented little creature.

Ray Aren't you happy?

Sal I am now.

Writer He was eight and I was five. We were sent to boarding school. He could do all the things little children have to do to become acceptable in the adult world. He could feed himself, tie his shoe laces. He had bowel control in the daytime and he was learning to read. He loves books. The head at the school had taken him to see a homoeopathic doctor regularly. They had to travel to London. They used to catch a bus in front of a bookshop, I can see him examining the window. He sees a book on King Arthur and the Knights of the Round Table. He wants it. The headmistress explains that he can't have it and luckily for her the bus arrives. He still wants the book. She holds him tight, she doesn't let go of him inside the bus. She knows that he is quite capable of leaping off into the traffic. He'll do anything to get back to that window. He is very determined and she wishes that he hadn't got such a good memory, he won't forget, because she dreads their next visit to London. He wants that book. He seems to have no fear, and he loves adventuring.

Consultant Y'know, I'd give anything to be an eccentric. Trouble is, I'm too normal, too damn sane. What might an eccentric do in my position? He'd give some hint, he might smoke cigars. That would be satisfactorily contrary to the clinical nature of my job. Like having a dirty overall on. I could fill the place with something. Bugs in glass cases, butterflies . . . Sheila!

The **Midwife** *enters.*

Consultant Sheila, what do I do that is eccentric?

Midwife Eccentric?

Consultant Me!

Midwife You could never be eccentric. You always park your car in the same place, you wear a handkerchief in your breast pocket, and you smell slightly of after-shave. Would it be eccentric to ride a bike to work. Or too trendy? Ecologically sound? You're not into politics, are you?

Consultant Good God, no!

Midwife That's not eccentric. How about a motor bike?

Consultant A big, flash one?

Midwife You could wear black leather.

Consultant On the bike?

Midwife Yes to keep warm.

Consultant What jacket and trousers?

Midwife Could be an all-in-one . . . like a cat suit. Zip right up the front.

Consultant You better send the next patient in before you have any more clever ideas.

Midwife I'm trying to imagine you eccentric.

She exits.

Writer He was like a part of me that would act and keep on tripping me up when I least expected. I was sitting on the steps outside the school when suddenly the calm school afternoon erupted, anxious people ran about with blankets and ladders; something awful had happened. My brother was busy exploring the roof of the old barn, trouble was, he'd climbed up and got too scared to come down, and the roof was too fragile to take an adult's weight. They coaxed him down eventually, but everyone was cross and scared, and I, being five, felt it was all somehow my fault. We were only two children who'd been left to look after each other. When Mum came to see us, she complained that we had learnt to bicker. I spoke always with my hand covering my mouth, and she complained to my dad that I needed his discipline. We both loved stories. We escaped into stories; we were always somewhere else. And we played games, well, I did, I don't think the kids I played with let him join our gang. He was too odd and the big boys left him alone too, but it must have left him feeling isolated.

The **Midwife** *returns with* **Sal** *and* **Ray**.

Consultant Hallo. Ms Wringer?

Sal Yes. This is Ray. My partner.

Consultant Oh good. How do you do!

Sal You said he should come.

Consultant And I'm jolly glad. We've got rather a difficult decision to make, so I think it is generally a good thing that he is here.

Ray I wanted to be here before but I was relegated to the chairs and the corridor.

Sal Decision?

Consultant Yes. We've had the results of that test we took, if you remember.

Sal Oh.

Ray You didn't say you had tests.

Midwife They are routine.

Consultant We offer them to everyone. They act as a screen, all they do is indicate that perhaps there is a need for another test. And that is about the size of it.

Ray You need to test her again?

Consultant Yes.

Sal Not more blood?

Midwife No.

Ray What's it for?

Consultant There is a faint possibility that your baby might have a chromosome abnormality.

Ray A chromosome abnormality?

Midwife What's called a genetic defect.

Sal (*panicked.*) What do you mean?

Ray Is something wrong with it? Multiple sclerosis? Hole in the heart? We saw it just now. It's got everything it needs.

Sal It was beautiful.

Consultant Don't panic. There is no indication that anything is wrong, we just want to make absolutely sure. I'll explain: when we measured the alpha fetoprotein in Ms Wringer's blood, the count was low. Now it has been found that, when this happens, there is some possibility of the baby being born with Down's Syndrome . . . Do you know what that is?

Ray I think I do.

Sal That man that sweeps up in Watsons.

Ray The looney.

Sal Ray, he's lovely.

Ray A lovely looney.

Consultant I think the modern term is slow learners. It's a physical and a mental condition. They are not capable of great intellectual achievements. But mostly they are harmless, gentle souls . . .

Ray What are the chances?

Consultant Very good, very good that you won't have one. Not as good as some people's of course. I had better explain. Trisomy 21, or Down's Syndrome, named after the man who first recognised the pattern, is a genetic mistake. There are many mistakes made, about fifty per cent . . . that is for every, um, correct foetus that is formed, probably another has been made and lost. The mistake that is made in this case is not, for some reason, lost. It's called trisomey 21 because what it means is that the genetic pattern in the baby's cells contains one chromosome too many, an extra chromosome on the number 21 pair: hence trisomey 21. I don't know whether you know that each cell contains twenty-three pairs of chromosomes. Thus.

He pushes a picture across the desk at them. Ideally the set should contain a screen or a blackboard on which diagrams that illuminate the text can be shown. The consultant would then be able to refer to the diagrams with a ruler.

Each pair is a different size, and contains a different number of genes. Now chromosome 21, as you can see, is the smallest chromosome, and it has roughly two thousand genes in it. So what I am saying is that a person with Down's Syndrome would have two thousand genes too many which is why the condition is both mental and physical. The pairs of chromosomes are formed when the sperm meets the egg, so one half of the pair is your genetic material handed on and the other half is yours. It's just that somewhere along the line the chromosomes haven't quite split properly. And if this had happened in any of the other chromosomes, because they are so much larger, the foetus wouldn't survive.

Pause. The **Consultant** *shuffles his papers.*

Now there is one other fact that you ought to know, and this is that this mistake occurs more frequently as a woman gets older. There is a relationship between the age of the mother and incidents of mongolism. For example, were Ms Winger to be twenty-five her chances of having a Down's Syndrome baby would be one in one thousand six hundred and sixty-three. She's thirty-five, so the rate is one in four hundred and seven. And if you were forty-five the risk would be down to one in twenty. Now the test that we have done has merely shown that there is an increased risk of Ms Wringer's baby having something wrong with it. That's all. I can tell you that there is a hundred to one chance that your foetus might have this chromosome abnormality. So that is the risk. A hundred to one. What you have to do is decide if you are willing to take that risk. If you would like to know one way or the other, we can offer you the amniocentesis test. If you accept our offer, then you will know exactly what is going on. Have either of you heard of amniocentesis?

Sal Sort of.

Consultant There is no need to look so worried. The chances are a hundred to one. You don't have to come to a decision now. The test is there if you want it.

Sal Then we'll know?

Consultant Yes.

Ray If there is anything wrong with our baby?

Consultant Yes.

Ray I see.

Consultant Sheila, how long can I give them to think about it?

Midwife A week, no longer. Since the Embryo Bill we've only got twenty-four weeks, not the twenty-eight. The trouble is with this test is that it takes up to three weeks to get a result.

Ray Twenty-four weeks?

Midwife Should the tests prove positive, which is highly unlikely, we can offer you an abortion.

Ray Good God!

Sal Oh!

Midwife And sometimes the test doesn't work and so we have to allow time to do it again.

Ray We don't want an abortion. This is madness!

Sal Ray!

Ray It is. I come in here to support you, and all of a sudden we are talking about abortion.

Consultant It's upsetting I know, but er . . . We are deliberately painting a gloomy picture. Filling you in on all the facts. We are looking at the worst that can happen. If your test is positive, the results show that your foetus does have a chromosome abnormality, then you might feel you want an abortion. There is not much point in proceeding with the test unless you are prepared to consider it.

Ray Sal?

Sal We can think about it.

Ray I don't want to.

Consultant A lot of people refuse the amniocentesis test on religious or ethical grounds.

Ray I don't have to be religious to object to abortion.

Midwife It'll be all right by us. Whatever you decide.

Consultant I do recommend that you find out all you can about Down's Syndrome before you come to a decision. If you feel, when you've discussed things, that you would like to see someone that can tell you a little more than I can, then we'll arrange it.

Sal Thank you.

Ray I need to get out of here. Excuse me. Nothing personal.

Consultant It is important that you make an informed decision.

Ray I don't want to make any bloody decision. Thank you very much. Goodbye.

Ray *exits.*

Sal Oh dear!

Midwife We get all sorts.

Sal He's sensitive.

Consultant Don't worry. Just let us know when you have made up your minds.

Sal *exits.*

The **Midwife** *looks at the* **Consultant** *and laughs.*

Midwife I think you are an eccentric after all. An 'informed decision'.

Consultant Well an informed gamble if you like.

Midwife If there is such a thing. Poor loves. You could lay all sorts of facts in front of them. Deluge them with facts but there is no way that their decision is going to be 'informed'. Whatever decision they come to it will arrive steaming with emotion.

Consultant I like the idea of black leather.

Midwife You're asking them whether they want their child – for better or worse.

The Writer The Consultant found himself wondering, as he so often did, about her sex life. She was so wholesome. Like brown bread and butter. So affectionate – with his patients, so wedded to the job, that he thought it possible that she didn't have one. And that seemed a shame, a waste. She would make some man happy. He half liked the idea himself, except of course he was married. And an affair with one of his midwives would be most unprofessional.

The **Midwife** *moves off. She doesn't hear the next speech.*

Consultant What do you think? Would you, could you fancy me in black leather?

Sal'*s and* **Ray**'*s kitchen.*

Sal Talk to me, Ray. Talk to me! I can't stand these silences. It's not my fault.

Ray I know I wasn't much use in there. It's a puzzle isn't it? Not what I expected. You know, I expected father of the baby, going in there, sharing it all. Not . . . Fuck it, hospitals. I hate hospitals! I was too busy sitting on my chair before being envious . . . to notice before, but . . . Never trust them. You just don't know where you are. Always springing things. Making life damn miserable . . . My cousin went to hospital once . . . swallowed bleach. We took him in terrified . . . Then it was all waiting, X-Rays, not knowing what was happening. They kept him in overnight. My Auntie stayed with him. She was sure he was going to die. Finally, they let him out with a bottle of milk. All those corridors, cream walls, and green skirting boards, the smell of the place, and the dreadful squelchy sound the nurses shoes make . . . They've got an investment in things getting worse, in illness . . .

Sal It's their job.

Ray Why do they always think you are stupid?

Sal He didn't.

Ray Ha.

Sal He was . . . It was quite complicated . . . He had to explain.

Ray And that midwife. I thought midwives were supposed to be comforting. She had a smile like a dentist's receptionist, no – a hygienist. I pity the poor bugger who pauses to think what she is like in bed. She'll have their willie off in no time and pickled, before they can say 'apple pie'.

He holds up a pretend jar.

That's a nice specimen!

Sal Jesus, Ray, that's not on. How can you be so sexist?

Ray Is it? I'm so sorry. I couldn't start to think about him in bed. Jesus, you'd be lucky to come out alive. All that stuff about finding out about it. God, who did he think we were? Sixth formers? Doing a nice little project on mongolism. That's what we called them at school 'mongs'! Find out all you can and come back for a gold star. He was so . . . oh so! . . . so goddamn fucking pessimistic. Ho, ho, ho, so you think you are going to have a nice little baby well I've got another thought for you. You just might have a hundred in one chance of having a cretin. Aren't you lucky? Why, why, why are there people in the world like that? Wanting to rub your nose in the muck – just for the pissing sake of it. You know what that man is? He defines the word 'spoilsport' . . . A referee that cries offside every time a goal is scored. One of those old men that can't stand seeing a dog peeing on the grass. A traffic warden. No, something really, really mealey-mouthed. Y'know, voice of gloom and doom. Sort of person you can never win against – Ian Paisley! Or your mother's friend Pete with the bad breath. You wouldn't want to be stuck in a lift with him.

Sal Finished?

Ray Yes. No. Mong, mongs, mongs! Look at that, Vicar, you've got a mong for a son.

Sal Stop it.

Ray I hope you are not expecting me to go along with all this bullshit.

Sal Just stop it. Stop it. Please Ray. Please.

Ray You're crying.

Sal Of course I'm bloody crying. So would you be.

Ray Darling, darling don't cry. I'm sorry. I wasn't thinking.

Sal It's so unfair.

Ray Lover. Sh. Sh. You were only just getting into having this baby.

Sal I want you to listen to me.

Ray Trust it. Trust it. It will be all right.

Sal *sniffs.*

Ray Honest. Look you don't have to go back to that clinic. I mean you only need your blood pressure checked at regular intervals, and loads of vitamins. I'm sure Dr Singh wouldn't mind if you just went to him. You like him, don't you?

Sal It would make good copy.

Ray What?

Sal The amniocentesis test.

Ray She can even pronounce it.

Pause. They look at each other.

Sal Sarnies?

Ray I'm not hungry.

Ray I don't want you to have this test, and you want to have it. Is that the long and the short of it? We're going to have to resolve this one way or the other. I am prepared for you to go ahead and do what you want. Provided that you don't expect me to support you and you don't hurt a hair on that baby's head.

Sal I'm making cheese and tomato

Ray I said, I'm not hungry.

Sal Suit yourself.

She slams down the plate.

Ray You are going to have it, aren't you?

Sal I haven't said so.

Ray That's not the point.

Sal I haven't said so. Supposing, Ray, supposing . . . Ray, we don't know. We simply don't know.

Ray Nothing is wrong. God's in his heaven and all's at peace with the world.

Sal You don't even believe in God.

Ray I do now.

Sal Bastard.

Ray Let's not fight. Sal?

Sal I know you're right.

Ray What's important is us. We must trust each other.

Sal Sarnies?

Writer I hear him talking to himself. He talked all the time. You could hear him. He had imaginary friends that he talked to. They played games together, and he used them to take the blame. Squeaky, Squeaky is his closest make-believe friend and scapegoat. I hear him blaming Squeaky, his voice rising. Whenever he did anything wrong it was always Squeaky's fault. Once, Squeaky got into the engine of a plane we were on and almost caused a fatal accident. I remember bad Squeaky best because I used to find it so extraordinary that he could believe that anything was Squeaky's fault. That he could expect us to believe . . . I don't remember anyone telling him that Squeaky wasn't real. It seemed too cruel. I was never allowed to . . . I was going to say fight with him . . . the idea was and is impossible . . . always there is the fear of hurting him, of having hurt him. And, of course, he and Squeaky were close as that . . . He protected himself with Squeaky, and Squeaky became a barrier between us. There had to be something wrong if your brother preferred a make-believe friend to you. I was seven and he was nine when we were separated.

Sal *comes into the kitchen in her nightdress. She has had a nightmare. She sobs into a box of tissues.* **Ray** *follows her on.*

Sal Mum . . . was behind this door, and something to do with lilies . . . she was trying to speak and they came out of her mouth, and something was happening with knives that had to do with the door. I knew she was dying, and I couldn't do anything, except stand there, I couldn't open the door. It was made of white wood and she was behind it, so when I opened it . . . and I'm sure she was calling me except for the lilies . . . I wish I could have stopped it . . . I wish she could have spoken.

Ray I expect she is tucked up safe in bed.

Sal Oh please, please Ray. I want this test.

Sal *starts to cry. Putting her hands over her face and turning away from* **Ray**. *As though she wasn't talking to him.*

I don't know what to do. I don't know what to do.

Ray Sh. Sh. I can't have you frightened and scared like this. Have the test. Have the test if it will make you feel any better.

Sal *turns to* **Ray** *and clings to him.*

Writer While walking his dog. Walking and stopping to pick up a stick, throwing the stick, and stopping again to pick it up, and throwing it again. The dog barking and behaving like a dog should. The Consultant thought about Ray, the man who had walked out on him. It was an idle thought. Men are different from women. But behind the thought lay the conviction that men didn't know what day of the week it was, when it came to babies. Ray's reaction had seemed pretty textbook. How he might have expected to react himself, providing he didn't know what he knew.

Consultant I often think about a doctor in Derby. A paediatrician not a gynaecologist . . . Once upon a time there was a baby born with Down's Syndrome, and when the baby's parents found out that that was what was wrong with it, they said they didn't want anything more to do with it. So the paediatrician left instructions with the nursing staff in the hospital that the baby should receive nursing care only. And this instruction was pinned to the baby's notes, and the baby did receive nursing care only: water and a drug, and after two days of this the baby died. And then, when the baby was well and truly dead, a member of the nursing staff sought out an organisation called Life, and told them about the baby's short existence on this earth. And the police were called in and the paediatrician was charged with murder and tried in a court of law. During the court proceedings an analysis of some of the baby's tissues was made and it was discovered that the baby had other complications besides the straightforward one of Down's Syndrome, and the charge was changed to attempted murder and the paediatrician was acquitted. And there was much rejoicing in the town of Derby, because the paediatrician was well known and well loved, and the town considered that he had been victimised. He was a good man. I think about this case because sometimes I am not sure what is murder and what isn't.

Sal *and* **Ray**'*s flat. They face each other.*

Sal I am a journalist.

Ray You are a journalist.

Sal Yes, I am a journalist.

Ray What has that got to do with it?

Sal It's my job. I have to know things.

Ray Is that what a journalist is? Someone who knows things?

Sal No. It's more than that.

Ray You don't have to feel guilty. Have the test for the sake of it. You don't have to justify it.

Sal Damn you. I'm not justifying anything – it helps, Ray. It helps. Finding out. It makes it all more manageable. I don't know. This article will be based on interviews with mothers, parents, people who have brought up, had to look after a child with Down's Syndrome – and my research. No, don't say anything. You can manage whatever. I can't. Some of the stuff

I've found is wonderful. They've got glorious sunny dispositions. The Aztecs, or was it the Incas? – used to revere them as though they were gods. Some of it is scarey, I admit – the physical stuff, the disabilities that are associated with Down's – but it helps to know, to meet other women, women who've been there, and to talk to them – and meet their children. I saw one today. They call her Livvy, her name is Olivia. She was so funny, so joyous . . . You see, I think Ray, if the test is positive. I mean if the baby has . . . I could. I think I could cope. It would be all right. Please understand.

Ray (*picking up a book*) There's even a Penguin book! I feel such a shit. Forgive me, Sal.

Sal (*out front*) If that is untrue, a lie . . . I've no way of knowing if it is. Having a baby is not how I imagined it would be. I don't know how to feel. I'm so confused. To feel my body changing is so strange. It's as though I'm no longer in control of who I am. I'm Sal, and I'm a biological thing, imperative. This baby will demand all the love, all the strength, I'm capable of. I must be prepared to take care of it night and day – whatever happens. I feel as though I'm on a beach and far out to sea I can see a wave forming . . . this wave will be huge, and that when it reaches me it will tower over me, curl up and I will be able to see how it shines, how white and clear the crest is, then down, down it will come, breaking over me, enveloping me. Changing everything I am, everything I know. There is no escape.

The **Consultant** *and the* **Midwife** *enter. The* **Midwife** *pushes a trolley.*

Consultant I've been giving a motor bike some thought.

Midwife Oh yes.

Consultant I thought a Harley Davidson.

Midwife Oh yes.

Consultant What I want to know is do you have to wear underwear under your black leathers?

Midwife You do. Preferably two pairs of knitted combinations. This lass that's on next says she's a journalist, so don't go mentioning black leather to her.

The **Midwife** *helps* **Sal** *into her operating gown.*

Midwife Attractive isn't it?

Consultant How are we today, Miss, Mrs or is it Ms Wringer?

Sal Oh fine.

Consultant Sheila here is trying to persuade me to buy a motor bike. What do you think?

Sal Well . . .

Consultant I think it is because she thinks I'd look fetching in black leather.

Midwife Don't take any notice of him, dear, he's going through the male menopause.

Consultant Charming.

Midwife First of all we do a scan to see where the baby is lying. We don't want to stick our needle into the baby do we?

Sal Might you?

Consultant Don't worry. She's got a warped sense of humour. What we are going to do is extract a little of the amniotic fluid. You know what that is don't you?

Sal Yes, the foetal waters.

Consultant The liquid that your baby is swimming in. Whilst the foetus is growing inside you it is also discarding cells, and these old cells are what we are after. What we want to do is collect a few that still have some life in them so that we can grow them in a lab, and get an exact picture of your foetus's chromosome pattern. Incidentally, we will be able to tell you what sex the baby is.

Midwife I'll hold your hand.

Consultant Yes, we're ready to go.

Midwife If you do feel anything just sing out. Should be no more than a period pain. That's right. Squeeze tight. I think she is nervous, Doctor.

Consultant Have you been telling her stories about me?

Midwife He thinks I've nothing better to do than tell tales out of school.

Consultant There we are. Want a look? All over. Did you feel anything?

Midwife Sit tight. I want you to sit still for about half an hour. Then you can go home.

Ray *sits on his chair in the corridor. He tries to draw.*

Ray I could go out to the park. Stroll through the buttercups. Stamp on a few daisies. Have a ciggie or two. I could watch the little kids through the playground railings. Get called a dirty old man. You're an old man – a dirty old man. I could find somewhere to have a cup of coffee. I could go into a pub and have a pint. It wouldn't stop there – as you know. I could go and buy a soggy biscuit and a cup of tea in the canteen. I could count the nurses in the corridors. If twenty-five nurses go by, it means good luck. I could bite my nails. I could read a paper. If I'd bought one. Nothing I could do would stop me feeling passed by. (*To his drawing.*) How do you feel? Invaded? It's as though the whole of what I am is a fart. We are both farts. Y'know, I could learn to fart in tune – if there was time.

The **Midwife** *crosses to him.*

Midwife All over with. Why don't you come and have a cuppa with her?

Consultant I am losing my compassion. I know that if a couple come to me and ask, are worried about what is going on in her womb, and ask for advice. Well I don't want to tell them to go away and have patience. I don't want them to have a sense of perspective. I want to get that foetus out and have a jolly good look at it. I don't want there to be any possibility that there might be something wrong with it. Something that I haven't detected. I'm like a dog with a bone. Because I relish my choices. If there is anything wrong I can either attempt to correct it, or I can tell them to forget it and start again. The point is, slowly they are stopping being people. Slowly they are turning into problems to be solved, problems I can solve, as long as I don't think of them as people.

The Writer The Consultant went home to his wife. She was dressed in pale green, with beige shoes. She served him duck à l'orange with frozen peas and mashed potatoes. It wasn't that she was a good cook but she liked to take a pride. They talk about the weather and 'this and that'. Never his work. It was, it would have been considered indelicate to talk about his work, since she had made the sacrifice of not having children.

Act Two

The **Writer** *enters.*

Writer Part Two. The Consultant fondles his dog . . . no. The Midwife. She is sitting in front of her gas fire with her little son, they are playing lotto. Clothes are airing . . . Ah, I forget, summer follows spring so it's summer. And the midwife isn't a figure from a Victorian melodrama. She plays cricket with her son, and she laughs. She is slightly asthmatic, nevertheless she rides to work on a bike. Sometimes she sings . . .

The **Midwife** *enters. She pushes the trolley. When she stops she tidies it.*

The Midwife never has time to reflect. She is always busy. She's got her son to think of. It's hard for a single mum. She keeps going because of him.

Midwife I wouldn't give up my job, not for anything. Nothing to compare it with. Plenty of job satisfaction, mind you, that is reflected in the pay. That's the only thing wrong with it. Still those that will, will . . . and that's my weakness. I will. The best part of the job is symbolised for me by two sounds. One, the cry of a woman about to give birth, just as the baby's head is forced down and out into this world, the mother should cry out, an earthy, gutteral cry. And two, the cry of a new-born baby. The one compliments the other. They used to hold new babies up by their ankles and slap them till they cried. Now, I know that is barbaric, and we want baby to have a less traumatic start to life, but I still like to hear a baby give a good yell. To show me its lungs are working. That's job satisfaction.

Ray *is at his desk working.* **Sal** *enters, she carries some shopping.*

Sal Hallo!

Silence. **Sal** *takes a fluffy rabbit out of the bag and sits it on the table.*

Ray!

Silence. **Sal** *goes to* **Ray***'s room.*

Hallo, I'm back.

Ray (*not looking up*) Hi.

Sal At least say 'hallo'.

Ray *turns to face* **Sal**. *He smiles.*

Ray Hallo.

Sal Come and talk to me.

Ray In a minute.

Sal I've got all sorts of things to tell you and I've bought a maternity dress . . .

Ray Let me finish.

Sal OK.

Ray Put it on.

Sal *exits to the kitchen.*

Sal In a minute. (*She is discontented.*) In a minute. In a minute. What's wrong with now? (*Raises her voice.*) What's wrong with now?

Ray What?

He listens briefly. **Sal** *listens.* **Ray** *goes back to work.*

Sal Nothing. (*Gets her dress out, she starts to put it on.*) I'll tell you what's wrong. You are too short-sighted to see over your desk top. Pig-headed, boring . . . working. I work. I stop. I have tea breaks. I talk to you. I'm sensible. Normal, caring. I want to tell you what he said about my article. I want . . . Ray!

Ray *has entered the kitchen.*

Ray Yes.

Sal Oh! You're there. Will you do it up for me?

He does up the zip at the black of her dress.

Ray I've come to the conclusion that, in order to do a stegosaurus proud, one would have to have an intimate knowledge of its skeletal structure, and some understanding of the size and function of its muscles. Y'know, Stubbs dissected dead horses in order to understand . . .

Sal Good thing there aren't any dinosaur carcases lying about. I should think they would pong to high heaven.

Ray What were you saying? You were muttering. I thought I heard the murmur of a domestic revolution.

Sal Do you like it?

Ray Hm, very fetching. Look better when you've filled out.

Sal You never stop working. You're a workaholic.

Ray Do you want me back at my desk now?

Sal No.

Ray I want to please. You've just called me a workaholic, and I thought I was being friendly and spending some time with my lady. How did the article go?

Sal Brilliant. He said it was the best thing I'd ever written. What on earth do you see in me?

Ray Not a lot.

Sal I want to know.

Ray Seriously?

Sal Mm.

Ray Well . . . um . . .

Sal Ray!

Ray When I make love to you, it is the life in you that I love. Your sense of fun . . . I'd say humour, except that sounds as though we were drawing cartoons together not living a life . . . Your joy, energy, hold on life. Enough?

Sal Do you really mean it?

Ray Really.

Sal Sounds wonderful. Must be someone else.

Ray No, you like walk in life. Your reality is stronger than mine. I am up in the clouds . . . escaping. Daydreaming. Reality, for want of a better word, depresses me. You are all the things I ever wanted to be. Sure of yourself, nice, kind, decent, sweet . . .

Sal Enough.

Ray . . . hardworking, trying always to do the right thing. I don't know what you see in me. When you smile at me, I think, is she smiling at me? You say you love me, and I want to look over my shoulder. I think of you in sunshine. I am in shadow. The sun is in your hair, your smile . . . I'll start singing in a sec. The final touch is the fact that you are having my baby. That is the icing on the cake.

Sal I feel good about that now. Y'know, having that test has sorted things out. I feel good about it.

Ray Good.

Sal I want to say thank you for being so understanding.

Ray Anything for you. I've been meaning to ask you. Has it really got to be a girl?

Sal It is a girl.

Ray How do you know?

Sal You can tell with a piece of thread and a button.

Ray I never knew that.

Sal I'll show you.

Ray I don't think I want to know.

Sal Come on.

Sal *finds a bit of cotton and a button.*

Ray I don't care what it is. As long as it is a bit like you, I suppose, and not too much like me. Its sex is not important. I want it to swim and speak five languages.

Sal Hold it over me.

Ray I want it to have a brother or a sister, or both. I want it to have a rabbit, or a dog, or a cat, or a canary. I don't think it'll ever have a pony. My earning capacity is not . . .

Sal What about mine?

Ray Yes, yours might be up to a pony. It's going round. What does that mean?

Sal What do you think?

Ray You've just made that up. Whatever it did you'd say it was a girl.

Sal I would not.

Ray You would. To bamboozle me.

Sal They'll tell us tomorrow.

Ray Tomorrow?

Sal You are coming with me to the clinic?

Ray Shit.

Sal Oh Ray, I want you to come.

Ray But you say the test results are going to be OK.

Sal I want you there.

Ray I best get back to work. I've got a deadline to meet.

He moves to the door.

Have you ever wondered why, with all the huge variety of dinosaurs that populated this planet, they were wiped out?

Sal Ice age. Frozen out.

Ray It seems, well, wasteful, after millions of years. And they aren't all hefty and plodding and stupid like I was brought up to think they were, God must have been in a bad mood.

Sal Are you going back to work?

Ray Reluctantly.

Writer We were separated. Now as I write I see the word, words – 'we were separated', and they are matter of fact. I went to one school, he went to another. I stayed with one lot of relations in the holidays, he stayed with another. Now I begin to understand how much that separation hurt. Was I the princess and he the frog? If so, my frog had lived on my pillow all my life and I loved him dearly . . . until they separated us. If there was an element of choice in the situation I wish I'd known about it. I might have screamed like anything. There was no one like him in my new world. I got deeply into normality – other people's normality. The less I saw of him, the more difficult it was to fit him into the picture I was forming about what life was like. I was shutting him out, because that is what they wanted. It wasn't till I was twelve or thirteen that anyone ever explained anything about him – and then it was my elder brother who told me he was a mongol. It was something. But, oh God, they are right to describe the term as racist. It was a relief to know that he was something, in his own right, not a hurt part of me, but on the other hand I felt that he was even stranger, a creature from another planet. I discovered too that I had a cousin who was also a mongol, and later that I had an Aunt, so there was a strange shadowy tribe of them living in my family. Twenty odd years later I discovered the term 'Down's Syndrome'. Syndrome to denote a collection of signs or characteristics. Down because that was the name of the doctor who first described it in 1866. When I talked to him about it, he was unsure what the term meant. He asked me if it was something Queen Victoria had – after Albert's death! He is still unsure.

The **Consultant**'*s room. The* **Midwife** *shows* **Sal** *and* **Ray** *in.*

Consultant Come in, Mr and Mrs Wringer.

Sal I know it is boring. I'm always having to say this. Just because we are having a baby, it doesn't mean that we are married. We are going to be married . . . actually . . . when the baby is born. I want a white wedding and I want to find out what orange blossom is like. Sorry to make a fuss but it seems important, somehow, to get the facts right.

Consultant That's very natural in the circumstances. Now . . .

Sal I'm sorry, I didn't mean to go on.

Consultant Don't worry. Where?

Sal It's just that I'm nervous.

Ray Sal.

Consultant I've got the results of the test here.

Sal I'm nervous.

The **Consultant** *goes through the routine of opening a folder and looking for the results, he pretends that he doesn't know them.*

Consultant Ah. Yes. Not very good, I'm afraid. I'm sorry to have to tell you that the test has proved positive: there is an abnormality in the cell structure of your foetus. It does seem to have Trisomy 21. Down's Syndrome.

There is silence.

Sal Oh.

Ray Sal!

Sal *moves away.*

Sal Don't touch me. I'm sorry. I want time to think.

Ray We should face this together.

Sal I know.

Consultant Sheila, I think we could do with some tea.

Sal Sorry. I didn't mean . . .

Ray OK. OK.

Sal *takes* **Ray**'*s hand.*

Ray Is that definite?

Consultant I'm afraid so.

Sal There must be some mistake.

Consultant No mistake.

Sal Everyone says that, don't they?

Consultant They were able to develop more than one cell.

Ray It's all right, Sal. OK.

Consultant When you've had a cup of tea and time to take it in, we'll discuss what happens next.

Sal It may be all right for you, but it isn't all right for me.

Ray Sal!

Sal I want our child. I want . . .

Ray Please.

Sal I want it. I want it . . . I . . . This isn't OK. It isn't OK. That is all I meant. It is not OK. Just not OK.

Ray Sal, Sal I meant . . .

Sal I am. I have, I heard what he said.

Consultant All right Mr . . . er . . . Brown . . .

Sal I heard what he said. I don't want . . . I can't. I'm not how you think I am Ray. I don't want this.

Ray Oh God.

Sal Don't touch me, just don't touch me.

Midwife Sugar? Does anyone take sugar?

Consultant Would you like us to leave you for a moment? This is bound to be an emotional . . . um . . . time.

Ray It's a shock.

Sal Yeah.

Consultant Do you want us to leave?

Sal No. We'll be all right. Don't leave.

Ray Shouldn't we talk it through?

Sal Talk it through. There is nothing to talk through. They've just said! Oh God, Ray, tell me this isn't happening. It's a bad dream. I'll wake up. Ray!

Ray *puts his arms round her.*

Ray Sh. Sh!

Consultant Perhaps we should . . .

Ray No, let's get it over with, whatever there is to be said.

Midwife This is one of those times when no one knows what to say. Except to say we're sorry.

Sal Sorry!

Consultant What is certain is that no one plans – can plan for a moment like this. No one plans for a child that is not beautiful and as perfect in every way as it should be. On a mundane level, if you see a pair of shoes in a shop window and you set your heart on them, when you go into the shop you fully expect to buy them and if for any reason you can't – they haven't got your size or they cost too much, and you make do with a pair that are a different colour and in the sale, perhaps – then you are settling for second best. One doesn't expect to have to settle for second best when one is having a child. But there it is, it is very unfortunate. You are bound to be upset and angry. I think we touched on the choice that you could make, if you wanted.

Ray I don't want to think about it.

Consultant You didn't before. If I recollect, you left in a hurry . . . But one must assume that, between you, you came to some sort of agreement. That you've talked it over and . . . um . . . otherwise I can't understand why you went ahead with the amniocentesis . . . We thought you weren't going to have it and then, all of a sudden, Mrs Wringer rang up . . .

Sal Ms.

Consultant Sorry.

Ray She had nightmares. She was frightened . . . I thought at least if she had the test, then that would stop her worrying. I never thought. It was like just something we had to do. Like an insurance.

Sal I was right. I was right. I always thought something was wrong.

Ray I don't know what to say.

Consultant Now you know there is something wrong, do you feel any different?

Ray About?

Consultant Going ahead and having the child?

Ray No.

Consultant I suppose technically the decision is up to you, Miss Wringer.

Sal It should be our decision. We are going to be married. I mean we are the most important thing, in all this. It's what we want.

Ray We must both want it.

Sal Mm. The trouble is I don't know if I can cope. I don't know. I want with my head but my heart . . .

Ray The trouble is we both want different things. I don't know what the solution is. I don't like the idea . . . I don't know if I can accept it. I feel I've committed myself to this baby. I'll put all my cards on the table. I work from home. I illustrate children's books. I'm sure we can manage between us. If the baby needs extra attention it shall get it. I think we should go ahead and have it.

Sal Her.

Ray Sal is sure it's a girl.

Consultant She's right.

Sal No.

Ray We can have more children. We've always wanted a family. What are the risks of this happening again?

Consultant The same as before – to start off with. Except that we would offer you Corionic Villus sampling. This is something we can offer in the early weeks of pregnancy before the Bart's tests. We don't offer it across the board because there are risks involved: we take a sample from the placenta, and there is a danger of miscarriage. The advantages are that we all know the results very early on before, really, a woman becomes emotionally involved with her foetus. Nothing would be as painful again.

The **Midwife** *has gone and put her arms round* **Sal**.

Sal Ray is a saint, I know he is. He is a lovely, lovely man. So much better than me.

Midwife Take it easy.

Consultant I hope you, at least, found out a little about Down's Syndrome.

Ray I didn't think I would need to. She did.

Sal I thought I'd write about it. I wanted people to know. After all they are sweet babies. Not like people imagine.

Consultant I think you should bear in mind the fact that this baby could be anything. By that I mean that, although we know that it will have Trisomy 21, we don't know to what degree. We don't know if the foetus will be lightly affected, or if it will have severe physical symptoms in addition to the more usual ones. The best we can expect is a baby with floppy muscles, and generally looser joints than is normal. Most likely it will have an extra fold of skin over its eyelids. And probably a tongue that protrudes. That is the best you can expect – along with a low IQ.

Sal They call them slow learners. Not handicapped or sub-normal . . . slow learners. It doesn't make them sound any different. Their emotional range is the same. They are capable of love.

Ray You can't qualify what someone is by what IQ they have. It's like saying people with low IQs are less human.

Consultant They are less able to look after themselves.

Sal But they are not mentally sick.

Consultant You did do your research.

Sal I have to do things properly . . .

Consultant I find that a lot of people find the mental factor, the low IQ, the thing that fills them with revulsion and horror. People are scared of mental subnormality.

Midwife At least it makes the decision simple. I mean if you are frightened by it . . . We find with a lot of middle-class couples – it's quite simple for them too, if they are professional people, they have a very high expectation of normality. They want the best.

Ray I hope you are not going to start talking about second-hand shoes again.

Sal Can I ask something?

Midwife Fire away.

Sal What would you do? If this happened to you.

Midwife What would I do?

Sal If you were me?

Midwife I . . . I can't say.

Sal Why not?

Midwife It wouldn't be right.

Consultant It might influence you.

Midwife We can't give you answers.

Sal But you are both here, with us.

Midwife Yes.

Ray You work here. Your job is offering us the choice. We wouldn't be in this situation if it wasn't for you. We're here because you brought us here. And now you are not going to give us your opinion. Typical. Land us in the shite and don't give us a hand out.

Consultant I think it is right that the choice is yours. We are here because we have been trained to help you, to give you the relevant information. That's all. Science is about progress. We represent that progress. Do you want us not to inform you? Not to inform you about the progress we have made? Are you really saying that you would be happier if we had stood back and left you in ignorance, knowing that we could make this diagnosis?

Ray Yes.

Consultant I'm sorry.

Ray Yes, yes. A hundred times yes. You see, I want this baby. Surprising as it might be to you. I want this little mong. I want it. And what you seem to be saying to me is that there is something wrong with me for wanting it.

Consultant Have I said that?

Ray No, but . . . not in as many words . . . but isn't that what you are saying?

Midwife You can have another one.

Consultant This baby will have Down's Syndrome with or without our diagnosis. All we've done is find out for you. Medical knowledge is a wonderful thing. If you decide to go ahead and have this baby and, say, it is born with a heart defect, with a hole in it's heart, then we can operate, we can save this baby's life. We can help it through it's early years, when it runs the risk of being seriously ill with chest infections. We now know what vitamins it will need to keep its skin from chapping. We can even offer it plastic surgery. It's going to be a girl, you might want it to look as pretty as any other normal child. So don't knock science.

Sal It just would help us to know . . . what other people do.

Midwife Knowing won't help you to decide.

Sal Do you have children?

Midwife I have a son.

Sal What would you do?

Midwife I can't tell you. It's different for everyone.

Sal (*to the* **Consultant**) Have you got children?

Consultant No.

Sal Why not?

Ray Sal.

Consultant Do you really want to know?

Sal Yes, yes I do.

Ray None of this makes sense to me.

Consultant You won't like what I've got to say.

Ray I haven't liked anything you've said so far.

Sal Oh God.

Consultant It's all right. I'm not unreasonably insulted. Ask yourselves why. Why do you want this child? Why does anybody want children? Is it so that you can see the future extending indefinitely after your life? In which case this baby is going to be no use to you. Or is it because we want love? Security? A small person that is yours and yours alone. This child will be yours. That is for certain. You won't be able to find anyone else who will want to take her on. She will be dependent on you for the rest of her life. Or do we want children because we think that somehow they will be able to make up for all our failings? We will be able to take a pride in them even if we can't take one in ourselves. Do they justify our existence? Do we have them so that we have some one to look after us in old age? Or do we have them because we love children and their antics make us smile? I am asking you all these questions because I want to point out to you that there is a degree of selfishness in anyone's reasons for having children. And so that when I say to you that my wife and I decided not to have children partly because it would be difficult for her and partly because of our ideals, then you will understand. My job is all about helping women to give birth. The down side of my job is that mostly I help with the difficult side of childbirth, so I see a lot of suffering, a lot of unhappiness, but nevertheless I see enough healthy babies to affirm me in my convictions that unless a baby is really wanted – and perfect – then it would be better for that baby not to be born. People have always had babies in the past for the survival of the human race. Did you know that, since 1954, the population of the world has doubled? It increases by three births a minute. We don't need more children for survival. The resources of this planet are being stretched to the limit. My wife and I decided that we didn't want to add to this overpopulated world. This is what makes it difficult for me to advise you. I think there are too many babies being born, too many healthy babies . . . I think it is perverse to insist on having one that isn't, that will soak up care and attention. I tell you this because I consider you as adults who can think for yourselves.

Midwife Why did you say all that? You didn't have to.

Consultant No.

Ray Thank you for being honest. I'm afraid I haven't changed my opinion. Sal, the doctor thinks that we have a moral duty to have this abortion. I don't know about you, but I've had about enough.

Midwife Everyone is different, everyone wants different things. Some people can't manage things . . . It is no good being a saint if you can't really manage. Same as it is no good coming to a decision and doing something that you regret. All I'm saying is, don't be too hard on yourselves. We're here if you want us.

Sal Thank you.

Ray Come on.

Sal *and* **Ray** *exit.*

Midwife What did you do that for?

Consultant I seem to have been running underwater for a long, long time. I hate this job.

Midwife Do you?

Consultant Sheila?

Midwife Yes.

Consultant Can I ask you something?

Midwife What?

Consultant Why have you never married?

Midwife You can ask, but you won't get an answer.

Consultant No?

Midwife No.

Consultant Spoilsport. Please talk to me. I didn't say anything wrong. Not serious wrong.

Midwife You tried to influence them.

Consultant Well. What's the point?

Writer The Consultant was thinking that he would like to give up his job, his wife, his house – everything. Perhaps not his dog. He felt he would be happy walking the hills with his dog – forever.

Midwife Do you really want to know?

Consultant Yes.

Midwife Because I was the little girl with the pebble-rimmed spectacles and pigtails that everyone made fun of. I helped my dad in his market garden, and I helped my mum at home, and I ate too many sweet things, and I always wanted to be useful. So I went into nursing. Nursing is useful.

Consultant I need you.

The **Consultant** *reaches out his hand to the* **Midwife**.

Writer The Consultant reached out his hand to the Midwife, she looked at it. It would be nice to think he was serious.

Midwife No, you don't. You need an audience.

Consultant That's not true.

Writer He knew what he needed just at that minute in his consulting room. A double bed and the midwife splendid in a black negligé or without it. He wanted her soft body to rest underneath him. He wanted her to open herself and above all he wanted to forget, to forget everything. To forget that he was a Consultant, and the nature of life and death.

Consultant Those two will be back.

Midwife Do you think so?

Consultant I'm ready to bet on it.

Midwife I don't make bets like that.

Consultant When you go out for lunch will you buy me a bottle of scotch?

Writer His heroes are all figures of legend: King Arthur, Robin Hood, the great and the good. He loves things historical, English history in particular. He's a monarchist. Old castles, abbeys, stately homes . . . He's asked me to buy him some postcards of Stonehenge and Avebury. I must remember. He is studying the Stone Age. He used to make up plays. We would sit on the lawn and watch. All of us indulged him, like you would a child. Somehow we were ashamed and so we patronised him. My mother spoilt him rotten. She told me once that she'd been worried when she was pregnant with him that something was wrong and that she had driven hundreds of miles down impossible, bumpy roads to try to get an abortion. It was one of those stories that you can't work out if they were true or not. It seemed so improbable. When he was in his early twenties a place was found for him in a sheltered community. The day we took him there was awful. It was a Sunday, we went by taxi, and it poured. The village seemed deserted, we unpacked him then we left. It felt like leaving someone in hospital . . .

Mum had given him the impression that the arrangement was only temporary. He might have been on trial, but he had the impression that he could decide, and that one day when he was better he could leave. For years he talked about leaving . . . He lives in a Camphill village. It is a wonderful place, and he has been lucky, but he has also made his own luck.

Sal *and* **Ray** *enter their cooking area.*

Ray That's it. That's it, sweetheart. You are not ever going back there again. When you need to see someone, you can see Dr Singh. You can have the baby at home if necessary. We don't need them or their stinking philosophy.

Sal We haven't talked about this.

Ray Do we need to?

Sal We haven't talked about it.

Ray All right Sal, don't get hysterical.

Sal I wish you would listen to me

Ray I do.

Sal My baby has got Down's Syndrome. It's a mongol.

Ray Ours. Our baby, Sal. I thought you were basically all right about Down's . . . I thought the problem was not knowing. Knowing, we have to make adjustments . . . But at least now we know the worst.

Ray *goes to his desk. He returns carrying the baby folder. He puts it down on the table.*

Sal God help me! Ray please, not now.

Ray I thought it would do us both good to see her.

Sal No.

Ray She is still the same. As beautiful as ever.

Sal No, she isn't. I don't want to see her.

Ray She needs us more. That is all that has changed. We must get ahead, be more prepared. Paint her room. Ger her a cot and clothes. That rabbit won't keep her warm.

Sal Ray. Stop, stop.

Ray She must have the best. We must give her a proper start in life.

Sal No!

Sal *throws the rabbit across the room.* **Ray** *stops opening up the folder, although he fingers it.*

I can't. I can't give up work.

Ray You don't have to. You'll have to work harder. Write a book. A best-seller. I shall give up work.

Sal No . . . Ray, I can't. You haven't given me a choice.

Ray Sorry.

Sal I feel trapped. You've got it all worked out.

Ray I'm being practical.

Sal Yes.

Ray I always worried before that we would spoil our child. No danger with this one, she will need spoiling. There won't be any need for this child to be second best, not with a mother like you and a father like me.

Sal If I was an animal, if we lived in a forest, if we were foxes, or bats, or rabbits . . . we wouldn't bring up . . . we wouldn't waste energy . . . I know it is cruel. Evolution is cruel. Kittens. I had a cat, it kept having kittens, litters and litters . . . Mum would . . . she would drown them when she thought I wasn't around. The Greeks used to expose babies on the hillsides, leave them out overnight, only the strong would survive.

Ray Things have changed since then.

Sal What do you mean?

Ray We have progressed as human beings. At least I hope we have. Surely there are other things that are important now, besides survival.

Sal Such as?

Ray You said it: the quality of life. Affection, love, gentleness . . . What we give to each other. We don't ask for perfection from each other, we want love and understanding.

Sal I know.

Ray Well then?

Sal I don't know. All my friends have had their families.

Ray Yes.

Sal I didn't want a family before, not till I met you. I thought it would be so boring. The way people talk about their kids. Y'know, when they first started to talk and crawl and all that. Their whole life is their kids, and now they are all at University, or being brain surgeons . . . Ours won't. I don't know if I can stand by and see her suffer. They do you know. How can I stand by and see something that I love go through hell. It's perverse.

Ray We'll protect her.

Sal We won't be able to protect her all the time. And what happens if anything happens to us? Ray, I don't want this baby. I don't want it. Everything I've said before has been a mistake. I want everything to stay the same.

Ray Sal, it seems to me that we deny our common humanity if we deny this child. We become less than human, not more. How can anything be the same if we have to do this to keep it the same? I love you. I know you don't mean this.

Sal I want to have an abortion. I want to get this over with, get rid. If you loved me, you'd see I have to.

Ray *exits.*

Writer My brother was tucked away in a sheltered workshop. We could all heave a sigh of relief, and I could get on with life; parties, careers, boyfriends. Of course, he would always be there but in a special sort of cloudy way. He would be a reminder, a footnote . . . This was the choice that had been made for me, and with my agreement. I had lost access to my feelings for him. The part of me in which he lived had been crossed out, made to look unimportant, a mess. Something nasty to be forgotten. So I started my career which I gave up to get married and have children. No, I was never worried that they might be like him. As I said before, I was the princess, I'd been brought up to be a good girl, in schools where religion was important. C of E, one should make the distinction. And princesses have a certain amount of conscience. I think it has to do with looking in the mirror, and worrying that you aren't what you seem to be. At least Dorian Grey knew where his picture was . . . So, although I no longer had access to my feelings for my brother, I had guilt.

Ray *enters. He sees* **Sal**.

Ray You're up.

Sal *pours* **Ray** *tea.*

Sal Tea?

Ray Are we going to have an inquisition?

Sal I rang the clinic.

Ray Yes.

Sal They said think about it overnight. I have.

Ray I'm going to bed.

Sal It won't make a difference. Nothing will. I'll have an abortion tomorrow, if you don't want to stay with me. I would prefer it to be now, not later.

Ray So that's it. You don't trust me.

Sal Sixteen hours ten minutes, you've been out of the house.

Ray I want to talk to you about that.

Sal I've made my decision. If you don't like it . . . that's it. I won't be able to love her. It. I feel that it is my fault.

Ray It's no one's fault.

Sal Perhaps. But that doesn't help . . . I think it is mine.

Ray It could be mine. Think of it as mine. Have the baby for me. Think of it as my fault.

Sal What the hell does it matter whose fault it is?

Ray Please.

Sal I don't know what else to say.

Ray Yes, you could say yes.

Sal Except to say, I love you.

Ray When I set off for home the pavements were wet, which was appropriate somehow. Somehow fucking right. I wanted to sit down, stay in the quiet night, find a broken paving stone and crawl under it like some slimy great toad. Oh to be a toad in the scheme of things.

Sal Are we over?

Ray I've got to sleep. I'm too tired to feel. I'm going to bed. Maybe this is some terrible dream.

Sal Ray, I'm going in in the morning.

Ray Give my regards to your editor.

Sal No. The hospital.

Ray Wake me before you go.

The Writer The Consultant sits at his desk. He rummages in his dark drawers. He is feeling for the cold side of the bottle of vodka that he bought that morning. He has already had two tasters, or should I say slugs, or shots. It is half past eleven. He considers finding his toothpicks. He worries about the bits of bacon stuck between his teeth and bad breath. He doesn't want to upset his patients – unduly. He saw the midwife, Sheila, on his rounds earlier. He constantly sees her in his dreams. She told him that Ms Wringer had come in for an abortion. Winning the bet gave him little satisfaction.

Consultant Let us get back to talking about perfection. I wonder if we, as human beings, expect it . . . not a miracle any longer . . . part of being human. What we have will be, must be, perfect. Like living in an adman's dream. In which case what happens to . . . the garbage? Can we tolerate anything else? I ask as one who has long since begun to slide to imperfection.

The **Midwife** *is sorting* **Sal** *out. She is in bed, the* **Midwife** *sets up a drip.*

Midwife It is going to be a difficult day, dear. This is not like having a normal D and C, which is what most people have when they come in for an abortion. Because you are 22 weeks. We have to induce you, so you will be going through labour – a form of labour. It is a little faster than full term . . . I'm not upsetting you?

Sal No.

Midwife I am going to stay with you all today.

Sal Good.

Midwife We'll see this thing through together. Is your young man coming in?

Sal No.

Midwife Working?

Sal Yes. No. He . . . I decided to do this.

Midwife Good thing you aren't married.

Sal We might never be married now.

Midwife He'll come round.

Sal He won't.

Midwife We always find that men take this hard. They find childbirth difficult as well. You often look round and there he is; quaking in the corner. I've had men in here lying on the floor pretending it's them giving birth. Sometimes they get hysterical, well, you can't slap them and tell them to shut up, can you? In case they slap you back – and then you'd know all about it. Oh, I know, some young fathers are amazing . . . you should see some of them in here, helping their wives. Does you good. Help is the word though. Men help. Women take the responsibility. I don't expect your young man can see that – yet.

Sal He wanted to look after . . . it.

Midwife Very nice young man. A bit too sensitive, I'd say.

Sal He would have given up his job.

Midwife And you didn't want that?

Sal No. I felt like I was in bed and he was holding the bed clothes over my head. I was suffocating.

The flat. **Ray** *gets out the baby pictures from the portfolio. He places them so we can see them.*

Writer I used to have him for the holidays when my kids were small. Special weekends, never longer. Sometimes we had no money. That never made any difference; he had to have the best of everything. The days were filled with expeditions out, and treats. He wasn't to know that we didn't eat caviare every day of our lives. Although of course, in point of fact, he could never eat caviare – fish has always made him sick. Everything had to be absolutely perfect for him: blue skies, perfect meals – his favourite foods – my children, perfect angels, marvellous trips out, not forgetting magical trips to the theatre. I started to get migraines, I remember the first one vividly, we'd been to see Julie Andrews, he loves Julie Andrews, she was playing Gertrude Lawrence, I bought him a pink and white ice cream in the interval, it was disgusting . . . when I got home I had to go to bed. I was so ill the doctor was called. I continued to try to be the perfect sister, struggling to give him everything in these holidays – for years. I watched the headaches. But eventually, and thank goodness, the idea of being perfect in any department of my life began to wear thin, I was forced to ask him to help me. First it was with the washing up, and then it was by not having trips out, and then it was by being there for me . . .

Sal *lies on her bed.* **Ray** *enters. He clutches some flowers.*

Ray I've bought flowers to say I'm sorry.

Sal Sheila was right.

Ray Sheila?

Sal The midwife. Oh . . . !

Ray What's up?

Sal A contraction.

Ray What?

Sal You have to go through like . . . birth.

Ray Don't they give you anything?

Sal They have done. I still feel . . . something.

Ray Shouldn't someone . . .

Sal I'm all right. Hold my hand. Talk to me.

Ray What about? Look Sal, I'm sorry.

Sal Not about being sorry. About something, anything else.

Ray Oh.

Sal What have you done? Have you slept all day?

Ray No. I thought I might work but the dinosaurs looked too green, they needed a rest, so I went for a walk. I went to the forest, because we go there, and I thought . . . there might be some way . . .

Sal *has another contraction.*

Ray I went to the bit where it is difficult to get in. You know you have to scramble through holly bushes, you get scratched to buggery, but we like it for some reason . . .

Sal We made love.

Ray Yeah. I went to that bit. I wanted to find the fallen beech. You remember. We climbed up and you almost wet your knickers 'cause you were scared . . .

Sal I wasn't.

Ray I told you that there were probably thousands of adders living under the roots . . . Are you all right, Sal?

The **Midwife** *enters.*

Midwife Hallo there!

She goes to **Sal**.

Won't be long now. Go on talking.

Ray You should see it now. It's magical, all the leaves are out . . . it's like being underwater. The beech is like a great white wreck, and you can imagine octopuses and sharks.

Sal Ray?

Ray Yes.

Sal It's happening and I can't . . . I'm sorry. I'm sorry.

Midwife It's all right. Tell her it is all right, and bathe her face.

Sal I feel awful about it. Bloody awful. Bloody men!

Midwife Don't take any notice. Over soon.

Sal I don't want my face washed. I want . . . why can't you. Oh fuck it, fuck it, Oh!

Midwife Try pushing. Push.

Sal Oh God!

Midwife Hold her hand. It's coming.

Ray Sal, Sal.

Sal Go away, will you? Go away . . .

Midwife All over with.

Sal Shit! Shit!

Ray It's alright, Sal. Hold hard. All right. Over with.

Midwife Try and relax, lovey, try and relax.

Sal Forgive me? Do you forgive me?

Sal *starts to cry.* **Ray** *holds her.*

Sal Tell me about your walk in the forest, tell me. Again. Again. Tell me again.

Ray Well, I felt like going for a long walk. The dinosaurs were getting to me. I was seeing dinosaurs. Their huge bones and their fangs. I see them only in terms of the books . . . I think I will have to spend some time in the Natural History Museum and mug them up. So I took the car and drove to the forest . . .

The **Midwife** *holds a bundle.*

Midwife I am going to ask you if you want to see the baby. You can hold her if you like. We find it helps. The hospital will photograph her for you, so that you can have a reminder, and you might want to make special arrangements for the burial. You might like to know that there is a support group. It is called 'Support after Termination for Abnormality'. There are other people you can talk to who have been through this. It's a comfort. The important thing to remember is that it is a death. You have to accept that. The death of a dream, if you like. I'm sorry. I can't help blubbing like a two-year-old.

The **Consultant** *enters.*

Consultant She's human too. Here.

He gives the **Midwife** *his handkerchief.*

How are we? All over with?

Sal Yes.

Consultant There. There. You're bound to get a little weepy now and then. Make sure you can take care of her. She needs feeding up, and keeping warm. She shouldn't do too much too soon. Someone needs to tell the friends and relations. It is perfectly all right if you want to tell them that you have had a miscarriage, just leave it at that. Don't explain to anyone. You don't have to write anything. There is no moral obligation to explain – anything!

Writer Except he thought, to God, and he had given up explaining to God, a long time ago. He wouldn't, couldn't even, ask for forgiveness. It all seemed beyond him, and cynical. He had begun to especially dislike all those arguments and conversations about when the soul entered the body.

Sal *and* **Ray**'*s flat. They have returned from the hospital.*

Sal It was the oddest thing. The moment you put yourself in their hands, they surround you with kindness. Kindness I would have preferred not to have. They bath you and they shave you and they put you in a white, pure white nightdress. Boiled, with ties down the back, and you climb into a white, white bed. As though you were a little angel. Then they put you on drips, and give you injections and take your blood. And you keep thinking – why is this so nice? I never wanted this, never, never! The midwife – Sheila, the midwife . . . she is there all the time holding your hand. She is so calm and . . . 'This won't hurt. This will. Be brave. All over soon.' And it is over . . . like going through a tunnel . . . travelling. I feel I've aged a hundred years. The kitchen is still the same. You haven't washed up.

Ray Hot-water bottle, cocoa, bed!

Sal Was it such a terrible thing to do?

Ray It is all over with.

They exit. After a moment, **Ray** *returns.* **Ray** *goes to his desk and unveils his baby pictures stroking the head of the foetus with one finger.*

Ray Hallo little one, hallo! What a big head. Just like E.T. Did you know that?

He goes and gets his paints to continue painting.

I wonder how you feel now. Back in the ether. I've had a day and a night of it since I last saw you. Yeah. Not what I wanted. Or expected. You've got such delicate arms. Anyone ever told you that? And the bend of your knees, it's classic, and your tiny fingers. They said they would take a hand print. You know what surprises me? There you are so vulnerable, I think they thought of the word vulnerable with you in mind, but growing, programmed to grow, and to go on growing, unstoppable – except and unless, by drastic measure . . . You are not vulnerable.

Sal (*off*) Ray!

Ray Better go.

Sal Ray. Who were you talking to?

Ray Myself.

Sal I missed you.

Ray I'm coming.

Sal I need you. I feel like . . . Charlie Chaplin.

Ray Oh.

Sal You know when he is in that hut on the edge of a precipice. I'm panicking. Hug me.

Ray I must have hugged you a hundred times in the last hour.

Sal Hug me some more.

Ray You should be in bed.

Sal Come with me.

Ray More cocoa?

Sal No.

Ray I want some. Go to bed, I'll come.

Sal Let me stay while you make it.

Ray I'm only making cocoa. Not being unfaithful.

Sal Why do I feel you are?

Ray What?

Sal Being unfaithful.

Ray Guilty conscience?

Sal Shit, Ray.

Ray Shit! Sal, I didn't mean it.

She goes to kiss **Ray**.

Sal I'm a vampire in search of a feed

Ray *extricates himself.*

Sal I want a ciggie. Have you got any in there?

Ray Yeah.

Sal *moves towards* **Ray**'*s room.*

Ray I'll get them.

Ray *find his ciggies.*

Here.

Ray *lights a ciggie for* **Sal**. *She inhales.*

Sal Delicious.

Ray *laughs then turns back to his room.* **Sal** *goes to follow him.* **Ray** *stops her.*

Ray Not in here. No smoking in here.

Sal But you smoke.

Ray Not any more.

Sal Why not?

Ray Because . . . no, go and smoke in the kitchen, I'll be out of here in a sec.

Sal *moves towards the kitchen, then she turns.*

Ray Out!

Sal What are you doing?

Ray Painting. Please go. Get that bloody cigarette out of here.

Sal Oh for God's sake.

Seeing the picture, she retreats as if she had been slapped.

Ray Fuck.

He follows her.

Sal Throw it away. Get it out of here. I can't live with that. Ray. I can't.

Ray Don't come into my workshop.

Sal I'll know it's there. Please.

Ray I'll keep it hidden.

Sal Ray.

Ray I said I'll keep it hidden.

Sal I think it would be better for both of us if I go back to work as soon as I can.

Ray Don't.

Sal I have to.

Ray I shall be desolate without you.

Sal I think we should move. Look for somewhere else to live that's bigger.

Ray Bigger?

Sal I still want children. I want a family. Perhaps we should buy a house. I'm going to bed. Don't be too long. Remember. Dinosaurs are extinct.

Sal *exits.* **Ray** *goes back to his picture.*

Ray Dear Embryo. You are looking very blue and beautiful today. Almost the colour of twilight. I hope it isn't too lonely up there, among the stars. I hope they've got you well tucked up or perhaps you prefer to swim. Yes, I can see you swimming, neat and fast like a little trout in and out of the Milky Way. You've got beautiful heels, take after your old Dad in the way of heels. Tell me are there other poor aborted souls swimming with you? Are you lonely? Or are there shoals of you? I like to think of you playing games. Star ball.

Ray *destroys the picture.*

On a screen is a video in colour. We see the **Writer's Brother***'s birthday party.*

Writer He was fifty last year. Earlier in the year I went to spend a day with him, it was a glorious spring day . . . we had lunch together and a long, long walk. When I took him back to his house, I said I had to go. He said, yes but you need a cup of tea before you go – and he made me one. It sounds so simple. It is simple. He leads a full and useful life, useful to his community, and he is kind and loving to me, his sister. They say he will age fast now. Selfishly I hope that it is not true . . . It is the quality of life that is important to all of us.

The **Writer's Brother** *speaks on video.*

Writer's Brother For my fiftieth birthday my brother and sister took me to France. We went to see the places that were important to William the Conqueror. The place he was born was in Falaise in France. He was a bastard. One day his Father was in his room looking out of the window and he saw Arlette. She was a washerwoman and she was standing at the place for washing, doing her washing, and her skirt was pulled up so he could see her knees. That is why the Baron sent down to her, and Arlette came up, riding on her father's horse in through the main gates. She was William's mother. She was never married to William's father. Which is why William was a bastard, and the lovely Arlette had a dream. When she was pregnant with William, she had this dream. She dreamt that a great big tree was growing inside her, with huge spreading branches, and the branches went across France and into England. It was the Norman Kings of England's family tree. I like family trees don't you?

The Choice

Why did I write *The Choice?* The subject matter is very close to me so, in a way, I was bound to try to explore it at some time or other. Or was I? This play was always going to be painful to write, so, in a sense, it was much more logical to resist writing it. The fact that I did owes more to propitious circumstances – meeting Annie Castledine – than anything else.

I met Annie just after having finished an adaptation of Schiller's *Mary Stuart*, when my confidence in my ability as a writer was desperately low. I'd been asked to take *Mary Stuart* out of its verse structure to make it accessible to a modern audience. Although that part of it had been fine, and audiences had liked it and it had got good reviews, I was horribly aware of how far away I was from solving the stylistic problem inherent in the undertaking. I could feel Schiller breathing down my neck and I wished like mad that I had some sort of training as a writer, like a University education, and a year or so more on my script so I could invent a language, possibly a verse-structure for it. So it was good to meet someone who was able to generate confidence not just in my abilities, but in our abilty to work together. A year after our first meeting, I went to Derby – where Annie was Artistic Director – as Writer in Residence on an Arts Council Bursary. The main task of a Writer in Residence is to write a new play for the theatre/director that they are involved with. To do this the writer and director have to find a suitable subject for a play. Annie educated me in her work by inviting me into her rehearsal room and by encouraging me to read plays she was committed to. She also suggested possible subject matter for a play. I remember reading everything I could on Vanessa Bell. Would she be a suitable subject for a play? *Novel on Yellow Wallpaper* – could I attempt this? Finally I took the plunge and decided to do something that was entirely personal.

The outline of my idea for the commission started like this:

> Dear Embryo (this was the provisional title),
> When I was last pregnant I had the amniocentesis test done. I was between three and four months pregnant and the results of the test took a fortnight to be delivered. In addition, the first test didn't work for some reason, so I was well over four months pregnant when I was given the all-clear, the green light – it was OK to go ahead and have my baby. I thought then, what would have happened if they had told me something was wrong with my embryo? In a sense I was already on the production line to abort. But at four months?

So Annie and I had the subject for a play, now all we had to do was find what form that play would take.

Discovering the right form is almost as important to me as deciding what a play is going to be about. It is also something which interests Annie greatly and is one of the reasons I found her so helpful to work with. Form is not something that is arrived at easily, or at least it wasn't in this instance. It is difficult to describe exactly what I mean by form, but it has quite a lot to do with the way I approach my subject matter. For instance, I started on *The Choice* by reading everything I could about Down's Syndrome. In the course of this research I rediscovered the Dr Arthur case and was reminded that Dr Arthur had lived and worked in Derby, so that the case was part of Derby's local history. Dr Arthur had even celebrated his acquittal by going to the Playhouse. It seemed that the play had to be about this case, so I trotted off to do the appropriate research. (The details of the Dr Arthur case appear in *The Choice*.) I became increasingly anxious and depressed about the play during this period. The facts of the case didn't make for light reading. And, in addition, Dr Arthur had died two years after the conclusion of the case. It seemed to me that I could easily end up treading on people's toes, and that to avoid doing this would involve censoring my imagination pretty heavily. It was also depressing to think that at the centre of anything I might write about the case was a dead baby. I wanted very much to be positive about Down's Syndrome.

The other thing that affects the form of a play is any knowledge you might have of the space that your play might go on in. I had arrived in Derby at the moment that Annie had given in her notice, and it became apparent that Derby was not going to have another Artistic Director immediately, so it became important to find somewhere else that might be interested in putting on this play, possibly in conjunction with Derby, and somewhere that would want me as Writer in Residence. David Horlock was keen to have both me as Writer in Residence and the play. Tragically he died before either of these things could happen and Annie and I had to wait to see who would follow him as Artistic Director and whether they would still be interested in the proposition. Luckily Deborah Paige was, and I began to think of whatever it was I was writing as a play primarily for the Studio at Salisbury. It made a difference. I wrote a draft of a play called *I, Barrie!* Barrie was a character with Down's Syndrome who lived in a house with his mum and a couple called Ray and Sal. Annie read this. I can't remember what it was that she said. She ate – I imagine it as a box of dolly mixtures – in order to have the courage to tell me that she didn't like it. I think she principally felt that, in creating Barrie, I had softened our original idea. Audiences would be influenced by Barrie emotionally, so the play would become just another play about an underprivileged person. I cursed but I could see her point. I'd taken the soft option. I really like Barrie. But that is what directors are there for – to keep your nose on the trail. Annie did like Sal and Ray, and she liked the material I'd written separately about my own experiences. The form of the play was decided on then. It was going to be a play for a studio audience with Sal and Ray at the centre, the consultant and a midwife forming a circle round them, and the writer encircling them both. All I had to do was write it!

Claire Luckham has written a dozen or so stage plays. Her first play was *Scum* (with Chris Bond) written for The Monstrous Regiment in 1976. Her best known plays are *Trafford Tanzi*, originally *Tuebrook Tanzi; The Venus Fly Trap*, written for the Everyman Theatre, Liverpool, in 1978; *Moll Flanders*, an adaptation of Daniel Defoe's novel, for the Croydon Warehouse in 1983. Her most recent plays are *The Dramatic Attitudes of Miss Fanny Kemble*, written for the Nuffield Theatre, Southampton, in 1990 and *The Choice*, written in 1992, the winner of the TMA best regional play award.

Weldon Rising

Phyllis Nagy

To Mel

So if you ever felt something behind you, when you weren't even one, like a welcome heat, like a bulb, like a sun, trying to shine right across the universe – it was me. Always me. It was me. It was me. (Martin Amis)

Characters

Natty Weldon, *35. Distressed by his ordinary good looks. Adrift, guilty, obsessive. However, his self-effacing sense of humour enables him to fight rather than crumble.*
Tilly, *not quite 30, but older than she'd like to be. Pretty enough, which is problematic for her. Naturally curious and incongruously romantic.*
Jaye, *not quite 30. Very fit, clean and thoroughly gorgeous. Mean, caustic and not afraid of being unsympathetic. Not at all coy or girlish, but not butch either.*
Marcel, *stunning young transvestite without a permanent address. Very much a man. Not at all effeminate or mincing.*
Jimmy, *Natty's lover. He's everything Natty isn't: tall, beautiful, outspoken.*
Boy, *so beautiful and dangerous that no two people can remember him in quite the same way. Very young and unfailingly polite, even when violent. The sum of all fears.*

Weldon Rising was produced by the Royal Court Theatre in association with the Liverpool Playhouse. The play opened at the Liverpool Playhouse Studio on October 27, 1992. The first London performance was at the Royal Court Theatre Upstairs on December 3, 1992, with the following cast:

Natty Weldon	Simon Gregor
Marcel	Andrew Woodall
Tilly	Melee Hutton
Jaye	Rosie Rowell
Jimmy	Paul Viragh
Boy	Matthew Wait

Directed by Penny Ciniewicz
Designed by Ruari Murchison
Lighting by Jon Linstrum

The setting is Little West 12th Street, a cobbled back street in New York City's meat-packing district. Factory buildings that may or may not be deserted. Shadowy, all of it. One surface must be covered entirely by a detailed map of the meat packing district. The map is enormous, overwhelming. One area of the stage, preferably above street level, represents Tilly and Jaye's apartment during the first several scenes of the play. The apartment should not be represented naturalistically. What's important is the sense that the women watch Natty and Marcel from a separate space. It is the hottest evening of the year.

The music should be treated as an integral part of the text rather than as background noise. Therefore, it is especially important that the versions of the songs indicated are used in production.

Much of the punctuation used in the play is not standard and is intended to create a non-naturalistic pattern to the language. The play works best in performance when strict attention is paid to the specifics of the punctuation. Similarly, the use of capitals in some lines does not necessarily indicate an increase in volume; rather, it is meant to indicate shifts in thought.

Lights up on **Natty Weldon**. *He's in the street. He wears boxer shorts and a wool beret. He sits before an art deco vanity, the surface of which is covered by bottles of cologne. The vanity's mirror is pasted over with postcards. Open boxes scattered about. Clothes overflowing from them. A portable steel clothing rack, full of men's stuff. There is a walkman and two tiny speakers set up on one edge of the vanity.* **Natty** *douses himself with cologne from every bottle.*

Lights up on **Marcel**. *He wears something ridiculous, like a plastic dress and platform shoes, but looks dazzling nonetheless. He is meticulously washing out a pair of pantyhose in a ceramic basin.*

Natty I might have been beautiful. I think. In Morocco. Ann Arbor. Montreal. San Francisco. Brisbane. Detroit. In transit. I used to be a little beautiful in transit.

Marcel Marcel says: you were never beautiful. Marcel says: you're a liar. Marcel says: YOU STINK.

Natty *switches on the walkman. It's Led Zeppelin's* Trampled Underfoot. **Natty** *begins to unpack the boxes, hanging the clothing on the rack.*

Marcel Marcel says: shut that shit off. Marcel says: SHUT THAT SHIT OFF.

Lights up on **Tilly** *and* **Jaye**. *They observe the scene from their apartment.* **Tilly** *drinks beer and eats popcorn, totally fascinated by the proceedings. Empty beer bottles are scattered around them.*

Tilly He's very skinny. Arms like twigs. That's unhealthy.

Jaye I despise men with skinny arms.

Tilly We should feed him. Maybe.

Jaye He's way past the stage for feeding. Forget it.

Marcel Marcel is displeased. Marcel wants some quietude in which to wash her tights.

Natty *ignores* **Marcel** *and continues unpacking clothes.* **Marcel** *hurls the walkman and speakers onto the street. Music out.*

Marcel Marcel detests rock and roll. And queer boys who smell of marzipan.

Natty That was Jimmy's favourite. I used to be beautiful. A little. With Jimmy.

Lights down on **Natty** *and* **Marcel**.

Tilly Men are violent. Even when they wear dresses. Let's stay home forever.

Jaye *kisses the back of* **Tilly**'*s neck while* **Tilly** *continues to observe the unseen scene.*

Jaye Hold still and let me bite your neck.

Tilly It's too fucking hot for that. Do we have any more beer? I drink too much beer.

Jaye You don't drink enough. You're coherent when you're drunk.

Tilly It's 120 degrees and if I don't have another beer I'm gonna . . . ouch. Stop that. You're hurting me.

Jaye When you're drunk, you let me bite your neck.

Tilly You know, he's really very skinny. But he has a nice ass. WOULD YOU PLEASE STOP MAULING ME.

Jaye Sorry. No more beer. We're dry.

Tilly Liar. You're hoarding it. Under the floorboards.

Jaye Tough. No sex, no booze.

Tilly I can't believe you're doing this to me. It's blackmail.

Jaye Hey. These are the rules. I bite your neck, you get a beer. I rip off your clothes, you get another beer.

Tilly Don't be such a boy.

Jaye Listen to yourself. Since when did you decide to be celibate?

Tilly Since it's gotten so hot I can't think straight. Jesus. I need a drink. Please.

Jaye Bulldyke.

Tilly Flattery just won't work anymore, honey. Look. That silly drag queen is washing his pantyhose.

Jaye You've been at that window for weeks. Talk to me, Tilly.

Tilly I wonder what size he wears. I hate my name. It's withered. We got any more popcorn?

Jaye Pay some attention to me or I'll get another girlfriend.

Tilly I bet he wears queen-sized. Long legs. Yeah. Well. Who are you kidding? Nobody else would have you. You're a mess.

Jaye Fuck off.

Tilly No, really. You're worse than me. And you got no booze in the house, no food and you got no air conditioning. Why don't we have air conditioning?

Jaye I like the heat. It's unpleasant.

Tilly And why does this skinny little fuck keep packing and unpacking clothes? I mean, why doesn't he just trash them?

Jaye I'm out of here.

Tilly Oh yeah? Where you going?

Jaye I told you. I'm on the prowl.

Tilly I hate it when you're pathetic.

Jaye Okay. So I might be persuaded to stay home and hook you up to a beer i.v.

Tilly Don't go out.

Jaye Why not? I look good under lampposts. Cheap and sexy. That's me.

Tilly You might lose your keys. Then what. Then you'd be lost to the streets.

Jaye *turns* **Tilly** *towards her.*

Jaye You ought to get out, too. Come with me.

Tilly I can't. My hair's dirty. I smell.

Jaye Tilly. It's all right to go outside now. It's all over.

Tilly We should have helped him. We should have run out into the street then.

Jaye I'm not listening to this any more.

Tilly Why didn't we help him? Now look at him. Nearly naked and still trying to hide his bald spot.

Jaye *holds out a beer to* **Tilly**, *as if from nowhere.*

Jaye Whoops. Look what I found. It's a . . . Corona.

Tilly I knew you were holding out on me. Bitch. Give it here.

Jaye Fuck me first.

Tilly Were you always this mean?

Jaye Yup. Now. What's it gonna be?

Tilly We used to be civilised, you know.

Jaye Too late for that. I'll count to ten. One. Two.

Tilly I can't help this, Jaye. I can't. We watched a man die and I can't move now. I want to sit at the window and rot. And drink till I drop.

Jaye Three. Four. I swear, when I get to ten, this all goes down the drain. Five. Six.

Tilly For chrissakes. Just let me have the fucking beer, all right?

Jaye Seven. Eight.

Tilly Okay. OKAY. STOP. What do you want? I'll do it.

Jaye On your knees.

Tilly *drops to her knees.* **Jaye** *goes to her, opens the beer.*

Jaye Mouth open, head tilted back.

Tilly *complies.* **Jaye** *feeds beer to* **Tilly**.

Jaye We did what we could. We called the cops. We're not responsible.

Tilly Just . . . shut up and feed me.

Jaye *bends to kiss* **Tilly**.

Jaye What do you love more: me or booze?

Tilly Shut up. Feed me.

Jaye *kisses* **Tilly**. *Lights down on them. Lights up on* **Natty**. *He cuts his toenails.*

Natty One night's like the next. I'm indecisive. I don't know which tie to wear. I can't choose between Chinese takeout or pizza. I think if I cut long and hard enough my feet will bleed and I won't be able to go out. We'll have to stay home, but no. Jimmy's ready to go and I can't stop him. We argue. I choose my most unfashionable tie, hoping he'll be embarrassed to be seen with me. But no. We go. We leave the apartment. We're on the street. We're moving.

Jimmy *enters.*

Jimmy It'll be good for you. Get out and meet your peers.

Natty They're not my peers. I own a small business. I have customers. I'm not political. They're your peers.

Jimmy Dances are fun, Natty. Not political.

Natty You can dance. I can't. You know I look like Peter Lorre in *M* when I dance.

Jimmy You have no gay friends.

Natty I'm not good looking enough to have gay friends. You go. I'll go home and bake muffins. But please, Jimmy, don't make me go to a dance where I'll meet lots of boys who can't have sex, looking to have it anyway.

Jimmy You've become so unfair in your old age. A shame. Come on. Have fun with me. Like in the old days.

Natty Every day of my life is an old day.

Jimmy Natty, everybody knows you're queer. Even your . . . customers.

Natty Who told you that?

Jimmy You don't fool anybody. Besides, it's not like we skip down the avenue holding hands and singing Judy Garland songs.

Natty I don't see any reason to broadcast my sexuality.

Jimmy Yeah, yeah. I know this story already.

Natty Really. In fifteen years have you learned nothing about me? I'm discreet.

Jimmy You're invisible.

Natty I think you need drugs. Valium.

Jimmy Maybe I'd like to hold your hand. Walk along Eighth Avenue and spit at passers-by.

Natty You spit. I'll crawl under a manhole. Jimmy: I DON'T WANT TO GO. I don't do witty repartee. I sell lamps. I sometimes wear polyester. I can't dance and leather makes me squeamish. I don't vote. I don't go to bars. My only friends are miserably unhappy straight girls who hover in cabarets. We sing along to every show tune ever written and weep at last call. I've never done a popper in my life. I just . . . do you. Come home and watch *Now Voyager* with me.

Jimmy I need people. Music. Smoke-filled rooms.

Natty Fine. I'll smoke a carton of Camels for you. Just come home. With me.

Jimmy Be more dangerous for me.

Natty Love me for my cowardice.

Jimmy I've done that for fifteen years. It's time for a change.

Natty I'm allergic to change.

Jimmy We haven't been out as a couple in ages. The boys don't believe me when I say I have a lover. You ought to prove I'm not a liar.

Natty But I *am* a liar. I'm pathological. I lie about everything. I crave it.

Jimmy I've got to be with people. Men. Happy sweaty men. Pressed together. Dancing for joy.

Natty On the train this morning, I was reading something German. Told the sexy kid next to me that I was taking a PhD in German literature. Told him it was the wave of the future. He was impressed. Gave me his phone number. Would you like his number? I bet *he* dances.

Jimmy I don't want a catalogue of your lies.

Natty When I met you, I told you my mother was Sonja Henje. That she dropped me out on the ice in the middle of a double toe-loop.

Jimmy I thought it was a lovely image. I still do.

Natty If I lie enough, it keeps me healthy. But in order to lie successfully, one can't participate too much. In life.

Jimmy There's nothing wrong with selling lamps, Nathaniel.

Natty You call me Nathaniel when you're angry with me. You've called me that a lot lately. The thing about lamps is, as you get older, it's less and less flattering to bathe yourself in light. I replaced all the bulbs in the shop with 40-watters.

Jimmy I won't indulge you.

Natty And another thing. I'm really fat. Yesterday I gained twenty pounds when you weren't looking.

Boy *enters. He lights a cigarette, watches them. They watch him.*

Jimmy My God. Remember when you looked like that?

Natty I never looked like that.

Jimmy What a face.

Natty Sure. It's not dropped yet. Wait ten years and oh . . . a few hundred thousand cigarettes later.

Jimmy He smokes like he's waiting to be fucked.

Natty No doubt he is. Waiting. For sure.

Jimmy Are you jealous?

Natty I'm not in a position to be jealous. People like me are grateful for any attention paid to us. We're happy for crumbs. Morsels.

Jimmy You're jealous. It's fantastic. Come on. Let's go.

Jimmy *holds out his hand to* **Natty**. **Natty** *doesn't take it.*

Jimmy *smiles at* **Boy**.

Jimmy (*to* **Boy**) Excuse us. We do this all the time.

Boy What? What do you do all the time?

Jimmy Argue in public.

Boy I wasn't listening.

Natty All right. You win. Let's go. I'll cringe in a corner and watch you dance.

Boy Have you got the correct time?

Natty I . . . you talking to me?

Boy Yes. The time. What is it?

Natty It's . . . late. I don't know.

Boy Don't you have a watch?

Natty Oh God. Don't hurt me.

Jimmy Natty . . .

Boy Hey. Fuck off asshole. I asked you for the time. That's all.

Jimmy It's 10.45.

Boy Oh yeah? Where you going?

Natty That's really none of your business.

Boy Are you a faggot?

Jimmy Come on, Natty. Let's go.

Natty (*to* **Boy**) What does that mean? What kind of a question is that to ask a total stranger?

Boy You're a faggot. Right? I know you are.

Natty Listen. You've got it . . . all wrong.

Jimmy No he doesn't.

Natty Be quiet, Jimmy. Let me handle this.

Boy I asked you for the time. You were rude. I don't like that. I don't like you.

Jimmy (*to* **Boy**) Leave him alone.

Boy *advances on* **Natty**.

Boy Awww. Isn't that sweet? Your man's protecting you. I'm touched. I'm fucking nauseous.

Jimmy Leave my lover alone.

Boy Well. Hmmmm. And where does that leave us? I come out for some air. Want to see myself a little scenery. And all around me there are faggots.

Jimmy Nobody asked you to come here.

Boy What. Do I need an invitation to walk down the street?

Jimmy No. Do we?

Boy Smartass invert.

Natty Wait. Wait. Let's be reasonable.

Boy You. You piece of shit. What's reason? You can't reason with sickness. You can't talk man to man or nothing like that. Can you?

Boy *advances on* **Natty**.

Natty Please don't hurt me.

Boy *advances on* **Natty**. **Boy** *breaks up into hysterical laughter.*

Boy Oh man. Oh SHIT. I really had you going there, didn't I?

Natty I . . . I . . .

Boy HA-HA. You should have seen your face. What a scream.

Jimmy What the fuck are you doing?

Boy Go on. Get outta here. Have a nice night.

Natty You scared me. How dare you scare me.

Jimmy We're out of here, Natty. Leave this moron alone. You know, you're real pretty. An asshole. But pretty.

Boy You think I'm pretty? Do you?

Natty How dare you frighten me. You ought to be ashamed of yourself.

Boy But I'm not. Fuckface. Fuckface faggot.

Boy *pulls out a knife. It's a casual gesture, as if he's lighting a cigarette.*

Natty Oh God. Please. I'm . . . I'm not a faggot. I'm not. Don't hurt me.

Jimmy (*comes very close to* **Boy**) You're such an asshole, Natty. (*To* **Boy**) Get out of here. GET THE FUCK OUT OF HERE BEFORE I TAKE MY FAGGOT FISTS AND RAM THEM DOWN YOUR THROAT, PUNK.

Boy *stabs* **Jimmy** *repeatedly.* **Natty** *runs away.*

Boy WHO'S PRETTY NOW. WHO? WHO?

Boy *continues to stab* **Jimmy**. *Lights down on them. Lights up on* **Tilly** *and* **Jaye**. **Tilly** *applies polish to* **Jaye**'*s toenails. A radio report is heard.*

Radio Current Central Park temperature is a staggering 120 with no drop-off in sight. Temperature expected to climb to 140 by daybreak.

Tilly It's gotten hotter every night since that night.

Jaye What night?

Tilly Don't play dumb with me. You get laid and you lose your memory? You know. That night.

Jaye I told you. I'm not talking about that any more.

Tilly One day it's 60 degrees. The next day it's a hundred. Weather doesn't happen that way. Look. It's so hot the polish won't dry. It cracks. Like tiny faultlines.

Jaye It's cheap polish, Tilly. What do you expect from something I lifted off the discount rack at Leroy Pharmacy?

Tilly You stole this.

Jay Uh-huh. On an impulse.

Tilly Slut.

Jaye You're a fine one to talk. I saw you stealing fruit at the grocers. Apples. Oranges.

Tilly I tried to steal bananas but I couldn't fit them in my bra.

Jaye I don't know if I approve of this.

Tilly Listen. I stole useful items. I stole food. You indulged yourself. The theft of cheap red nail polish is not exactly defensible.

Jaye So. Turn me in. I don't care. I hear there's lots of sex in prison.

Tilly You never let up, do you?

Jaye Nope. Get used to it.

Tilly I used to have standards.

Jaye And then you met me.

Tilly Jaye. We're middle-class. We don't steal.

Jaye We're impulse thieves. It's probably an illness. Like compulsive shopping. Except we don't pay. And we can't afford to pay, anyway. We spend all our pennies to make rent on an unglamorous shitbox in a menacing neighbourhood. It's an illness. Trust me. God. I love it when you're on your knees.

Tilly I'm kind of dizzy. Is it possible to get heat-stroke at night?

Jaye Silly bitch. Do my nails. Go on.

Tilly I'm thirsty. And cranky. Jaye. Are we unhappy? Are we so unhappy that we steal to fill a void? My God. There are so many things I'd like to take. I'd like to run through the city with enormous shopping carts and fill them with everything.

Jaye I'd like to fill my shopping cart with multiples of your tongue. And maybe your hands. That way, I wouldn't have to hear you go on and on about this stuff.

Tilly Take me someplace.

Jaye You're already someplace.

Tilly I was thinking . . . a beer run would be nice right about now.

Jaye Okay. We'll drag out the carts and go shopping. Wake everybody up. Get wild.

Tilly But then I think, well, I really can't bear to walk past him. He's diminishing. Daily. I don't know whether to laugh or cry.

Jaye Why not both. If you hit the extremes, you'll eventually get to the middle.

Tilly You know what. We witnessed a horrible crime.

Jaye I really can't wait to get back to work. The office is air-conditioned.

Tilly We witnessed a horrible crime and we've responded by becoming criminals ourselves. We never talk to him. Why not?

Radio *static is heard.*

Radio The latest reading from Central Park is 130 degrees. An astonishingly rapid increase in temperature has been noted over the last half hour. The Mayor has ordered that all businesses operating within the five boroughs close until further notice. It's . . . VACATION TIME.

Jaye It's time to make that beer run.

Lights down on **Tilly** *and* **Jaye**. *Lights up on* **Marcel**, *on the job. Every few seconds, we see headlight beams come and go. Lights up on* **Natty**. *He sits at the vanity. As he speaks, he touches the postcards taped to the mirror, one by one.*

Marcel (*to the passing cars*) Marcel says: Stop. Come directly to jail. Do not pass go. Marcel collects 200 dollars.

Natty Morocco has much to recommend it. Sand, for one thing. And intrigue, for another. And of course, there are the boys.

Marcel Slow down. What's your hurry? Marcel can provide motion in the comfort of your imitation leather interior. All you need's a decent car stereo and a wad of cash to make Marcel a happy camper.

Natty And Paris, well. It's natural that I would be attracted to the city of light. I love places where I can't understand one damned word spoken. Life's a breeze then.

Marcel So much traffic and so little time. Boys. BOYS. Take a breather. It's hot and Marcel is sooooo cold. Marcel has a brilliant theory which Marcel will reveal in due course.

Natty Amsterdam. Now *that's* a city. The prince of cities. I could get lost there. I could. Lost among the blondes. Blondes love me. They don't take me for a coward.

Marcel Marcel's radiant theory is this: it's so hot that people are keeping to their cars. They mindlessly travel the same stretch of the West Side highway for hours so they can be in the only air-conditioning that still works. But oh, all my children, let me tell *you* what will happen when those cars fizzle out.

Natty I'm sure I was braver in another life. I just don't know which one. London. I stayed indoors and avoided the food. Jimmy had a splendid holiday while I watched the World Scrabble Championships. I've got to take Jimmy's ashes to Westminster Abbey and hide them under the coronation chair. I mean, who will care?

Marcel Oh my honey pants, all of you. Your cars will self-destruct on this particular stretch of the gloomy highway. In the sweltering heat you will stagger from the intensity of moiself. And Marcel will wait for you. With a pitcher of ice water and clean pantyhose. Marcel prepares for your coming catastrophe.

Headlights beam directly at **Marcel**. *He's ablaze in light.*

Marcel THAT'S RIGHT, HON. COME CLOSER. CONSUME ME.

Headlights disappear.

Marcel Shitshitshit. Marcel's gonna collapse from boredom. Marcel's gonna starve and faint from lack of nourishment. (*Turning his attention to* **Natty**.) Excuse me, Charles Atlas.

Natty Brave. Braver. Bravest. Seattle. Salt Lake City. Cincinnati.

Marcel Marcel said: PARDON MOI MR FUCKING UNIVERSE. Marcel would like some food. Marcel would like *you* to provide hors d'oeuvres.

Natty You broke my music. You scream at me. And you want me to *feed* you?

Marcel You've invaded Marcel's space. And now you must PAY UP. Food. Glorious food. That is Marcel's desire.

Natty I have clothes. I can give you a hat. Or a necktie.

Marcel Marcel says: you are a silly queen. Marcel says: my splendiferous wardrobe is quite complete. AND WHO NEEDS CLOTHES IN THIS AWFUL HEAT.

Natty Courage is a state of mind. A state. Connecticut. California. Calgary.

Marcel You are depriving Marcel of a livelihood. Potential clients take one look at the skinny buttless wonder of you and they FLEE. Marcel holds you personally responsible. Marcel finds it a DISGUSTING PERVERSION when moneyed queer boys take to the streets. GET OUT. YOU ARE ECLIPSING THE SUN THAT SPELLS M-A-R-C-E-L.

Natty I haven't eaten for weeks. I think.

Marcel Marcel commands you to return to your hovel and whip up some . . . RATA-TOUILLE.

Natty Why doesn't Marcel go *home* and cook up some . . . RATATOUILLE?

Marcel *Nature* is Marcel's home. *Nature* nourishes Marcel. When it rains, Marcel's slender neck drifts elegantly back, Marcel's perfect lips part, and the *rain* feeds Marcel. And sometimes Marcel is nourished by unsuspecting gay boys who stay too long on Marcel's nature preserve.

Natty I must unpack Jimmy's clothing. I must make contributions to charity.

Marcel Charity begins at home. Charity begins at night. Charity begins with Marcel. Nourish Marcel. NOW.

Natty Jimmy always said you were sad.

Marcel Marcel has serviced the needs of . . . of . . . Neanderthal, Cro-Magnon and Renaissance man. Marcel does not recall a Jimmy man.

Natty Marcel watched him die.

Headlight beams swing by. A constant stream of light that suggests a mass exodus.

Marcel Take a break oh all my weary travellers. The night sky burns your eyes, but Marcel has a magic balm. Marcel is but a reflection of the company he keeps. Stop. STOP. TWO ROADS DIVERGED ON A HIGHWAY AND I COMMAND YOU TO TAKE THE ONE THAT LEADS TO ME.

Headlights disappear. **Marcel** *returns to his ceramic basin. Takes many pantyhose from his purse and washes them carefully. He lays them out on the street to dry.*

Natty A thousand years ago, when I was a boy and still had hair, I lived above a club on the highway called 10 West. At the time, I was a pharmacist's assistant. I wore white smocks to convince myself I was a professional. At night, I locked myself into my studio apartment and fantasised to the thumping and throbbing music that vibrated beneath my feet. One night, I stood before a mirror and combed my hair for three hours. Beneath me, Donna Summer and Sylvester wailed on. That night, I unlocked my door and entered paradise. I drank a vodka tonic and cried at the bar. Nobody talked to me. I figured it was because in my haste to leave locked doors behind me, I forgot to remove my pharmacist assistant's white smock. On my ninth vodka tonic, I met Jimmy. He tapped me on my shoulder and asked if I was a doctor. I said, no. I'm Natty. He said, so you are. So you are.

Music in: Johnny Come Home, *(Fine Young Cannibals).*

Headlights beam directly at **Marcel**.

Marcel A PENNY FOR YOUR THOUGHTS, SWEET THING.

Headlights disappear.

Natty Natty says: Marcel can use Natty's clothing rack. For the pantyhose. So they dry.

Marcel You wearing that ugly beret because you're bald?

Natty No. No. I have some hair. Some.

Marcel Marcel's tits are melting from the heat and you've got this . . . woollen monstrosity . . . perched on your head. You're sick.

Natty I'm modest.

Marcel Then do us a favour and cover that mass of undernourishment you call a body. Marcel is not comfortable around starvation.

Natty I shaved off all my body hair.

Marcel How nice for you. Marcel knows all about that kind of thing so please spare Marcel the details.

Natty I'm swimming to England. I've got to bring Jimmy's ashes to Westminster Abbey.

Marcel Marcel believes we are living in the age of supersonic transport. So you ought to grow back your leg hair and FLY.

Natty I'm not afraid of flying. But I fear water. So I must . . . swim. Brave. Braver. Bravest.

Marcel Marcel thought you were harmless. Marcel thought your major problem was that you smelled like an almond. But Marcel is no longer so sure. And . . . WHERE IS THAT DIZZY FAGGOT MUSIC COMING FROM?

Natty It's the lesbians above the poultry market. They like to dance.

Marcel There are DYKES in this neighbourhood?

Natty Uh-huh. They're very cute. Serious types. I think they drink a lot.

Marcel Well. Marcel says: this is BOYS' TOWN, honey. Marcel says: this is not the neighbourhood for LADIES' HOUR.

Natty You've never seen them? Dragging groceries and laundry behind them? They do an awful lot of laundry.

Marcel No fucking way. Marcel converses with MEN.

Natty Marcel never talked to me. Marcel never talked to Jimmy.

Marcel Listen here, Mister Sandman. Marcel can spot those who are worth conversing with. Marcel knows a dud when Marcel spots one. LISTEN UP MY LEZZIE SISTERS: CUT THE FUCKING MUSIC. DANCE TO YOUR OWN DIFFERENT FUCKING DRUMMER BUT LEAVE MARCEL OUT OF IT.

Music gets louder.

Marcel Marcel speaks and the whole world DOESN'T LISTEN. Marcel regrets that Marcel was forced to converse with unseen womanhood. But that is the way the cookie crumbles here in the meat market.

Natty You never talked to me. You never talked to Jimmy while he was bleeding to death in your own backyard.

Music out.

Marcel Sigh. Oh my ridiculous shrinking boy child. SIGH. Marcel sighs a big sigh as Marcel recalls the flight of this pathetic boy child one night not too long ago when there was blood on the cobblestones and on his chicken-little hands. Marcel saw all. Marcel speaks THE TRUTH. What were you doing, sweat pea? Where were *you* running to? Marcel says: end of fairy tale.

Natty Courage. Courage in the face of adversity. Danger. Grab the danger by its horns and ride it. Ride it. I don't. I don't. I don't wanna die. I am. I am. I am . . . dangerous. I am dangerous and I am . . . NATTY. I AM NATTY. So you are, he said. So you are. He swept me off my earthbound feet and it was many years later I betrayed him.

Music in: You Make Me Feel (Mighty Real), (*Sylvester*). **Jimmy** *enters. He dances as if he's dancing in a crowd, all smiles and sweat. He's doing poppers.* **Marcel** *is awe-struck by this apparent apparition.*

Natty Then as now, I wouldn't dance with him. Old habits die hard. But he danced for me. There's nothing sexier than watching somebody dance for you. We were so young and so happy. His body a dazzling intricacy of muscle and smoothness. His hands yet unblemished by stress, work, heartbreak. Jimmy. Your body was a testament to youth and so was mine in its half-assed way. The importance we attach to our bodies. They are ephemeral. We are ephemeral and if I could have danced with you that night I would have told you so. Bodies are unimportant until we lose them.

Jimmy Natty Weldon. Watch me dance for you.

Natty I'm watching, Jimmy. I'm always watching.

Jimmy Let's grow up and become Senators. Diplomats.

Natty *approaches* **Jimmy**

Natty Let's *not* grow up and avoid the mess.

Jimmy I like mess. The stuff of life. I'm a dancing fool.

Jimmy *continues to dance.* **Natty** *is motionless, close to him.*

Natty Beautiful people are allowed to be fools. They can even dance. But the less beautiful are left running after departing trains. Missed connections. You're beautiful, Jimmy.

Jimmy Someday my prince will come and his name will be Nathaniel. Someday we'll be 75 and rail at the indecency of the younger generation. At the old gay home, poppers will be fed to us intravenously and Bette Midler will do the New Year's Eve show.

Natty How old are you, Jimmy?

Jimmy I'm 20 years old and I am HOT. Come on. Let me take you on a fast train to meet my folks.

Natty I'm a coward.

Jimmy This is the seventies. There's no room for cowardice.

Natty I was never 20 years old. I'm tired. Jimmy. What if I told you that in 15 years I will betray you. What if I told you that I will run from you when it counts most. What if I told you that in 15 years I will watch you die. What then?

Jimmy *takes* **Natty** *into his arms.*

Jimmy There's always the hope that you won't run. The next time.

Natty There's never a next time, Jimmy.

Jimmy Everywhere you look there's a next time.

Boy *enters. Music out.*

Boy Are you a faggot?

Jimmy (*to* **Natty**) Tell me what you'll do. Next time.

Natty I . . . I . . .

Boy You. YOU. Ugly man. Jerkoff. Fuckface. I smell the fear on you. HATE YOURSELF FOR ME. Show me you know what I mean. WHO ARE YOU, BOY?

Natty I'm . . . I'm . . .

Jimmy Hold me close and tell me who you are. Take me places and show me that we will be legion, marching in rows as far as the eye can see and we are all telling each other who we are. Over and over.

Natty I'm . . . I'm . . .

Boy It doesn't matter how I get you. In the end I'll get you all. I'll crush you under my heel because YOU CAN'T TELL ME WHO YOU ARE.

Natty I'm. Natty.

Jimmy So you are. So you are.

Jimmy *and* **Natty** *kiss.* **Boy** *pulls out a knife.* **Marcel** *drops to the ground, covering his head with his hands. Lights up on* **Tilly** *and* **Jaye**, *who watch from their apartment.*

Tilly He's got a knife. He's gonna use it.

Jaye Get away from the window.

Marcel Pleasepleaseplease don't look at me. Don't look at me. Don't look at me.

Boy You think I'm pretty? How pretty am I? Tell me.

Natty You ought to be ashamed of yourself.

Boy But I'm not. I'm taller and prouder and PRETTIER than you.

Tilly Should we scream or something? I don't know, to chase him away?

Jaye Get away from the window.

Marcel I don't wanna be cut. No cuts. No bruises. NO CUTS. Go awaygoawayaway.

Natty Let's be reasonable. Talk sense.

Jimmy He's not reasonable, Natty.

Boy I'm not reasonable.

Natty You've got a future. It's bright. Put down the knife and talk to us.

Jimmy He's not reasonable, Natty.

Boy I'm not reasonable. I'm PRETTY.

Tilly Let's do something.

Jaye Why should we?

Marcel Marcel does not want to see this. Marcel says: NO.

Boy Faggot. You disgust me. You crowd my world.

Natty I'm . . . I'm . . .

Jimmy Hold me close. Hold on.

Boy GET OUTTA MY NEIGHBOURHOOD.

Natty I'm . . . I . . . CAN'T.

Boy *stabs* **Jimmy** *repeatedly.*

Boy WHO'S PRETTY NOW. WHO? WHO?

Natty *runs away.* **Boy** *runs away.* **Marcel** *rises to look at the carnage.* **Jaye** *joins* **Tilly** *at the window.*

Jaye Call the police.

Tilly Okay.

Jaye It's so . . . quiet.

Tilly Yeah. We better call the cops.

Jaye Okay.

A silence, as **Marcel, Jaye** *and* **Tilly** *look at* **Jimmy**. *Headlights beam directly at* **Marcel**. *Lights down on all but* **Marcel**.

Marcel HEY. COME AND SIT WITH ME A WHILE. YOU DON'T EVEN GOT TO PAY. BE WITH ME. BE WITH ME.

Headlights disappear. Light up on **Natty** *at the vanity. Throughout the following scene, he very carefully removes the postcards from the mirror, cuts them up into tiny pieces, and throws them to them wind.*

Natty We'll never forget, will we, Marcel?

Marcel What are you talking about silly gay boy? WHAT?

Natty Where are you from, Marcel? Where is that place that lets you forget?

Marcel Marcel is a citizen of the universe. Marcel forgets nothing. However, Marcel does employ considerable editing skills. From time to time.

Natty Sometimes I think I'll be fine in the end. That I'll wake up in the morning and be able to get through the day without telling myself even one lie. But you know, just *thinking* that it's gonna be okay in the end is a lie. So. Where does *that* leave us?

Tilly *and* **Jaye** *enter the street. They drag a shopping cart with them. It's full of beer.*

Marcel My, my. If it isn't the luscious lushes of Little West 12th Street.

Jaye Fuck off, freak.

Tilly Jaye, *really*. (*To* **Marcel**.) Hi. I'm Tilly. This is Jaye. And this is our beer. I think we almost met you at the police station.

Jaye Yeah. You were looking particularly Jayne Mansfield-esque that morning.

Marcel Marcel says: lesbians have no manners.

Natty Hi. I'm Natty. I'm a liar.

Tilly Oh, great. So are we.

Natty Really.

Tilly Sure. We lie all the time. About most everything.

Jaye We steal, too. We stole this beer.

Marcel Marcel wants nothing to do with petty thieves.

Jaye Aren't you an anachronism?

Natty This is Marcel. Marcel . . . hovers.

Jaye Why do you refer to yourself in the third person, Marcel?

Marcel Marcel IS the third person.

Jaye Heat-stroke. Transvestite clown succumbs to heat-stroke. Melted down in the prime of womanhood. A sad, sad story.

Natty Did you really steal that beer?

Tilly Yeah. You ought to see it out there. It's wild. Not a soul in the streets. Supermarkets deserted. Restaurants abandoned. But the cars. Wow. More cars than I've ever seen packed together like . . . like butane lighters waiting to explode.

Jaye We need the beer 'cause we ain't got air-conditioning.

Natty I'm trying to be courageous. And everyone's gone. Nobody to watch me spit at passers-by.

Tilly We're here. You want a beer? I think we almost met you at the police station, too.

Natty I was the one with the bag over my head, crouching in a corner. If you don't mind, I'll trade you some perfume for a beer.

Jaye Looks like we're having a block party.

Jaye *removes a small portable radio from the shopping cart.*

Marcel Marcel must return to work. Marcel has no time for parties.

Jaye Haven't you heard? They've cancelled work.

Marcel *Who* cancelled work?

Jaye The big deals. The men in suits. Though I doubt they're wearing suits at this moment.

Jaye *turns on the radio. Static. More static. Then:*

Radio . . . schools, banks, post offices closed. Subway and bus service has been suspended. Current Central Park temperature 143 degrees. A rapid increase in temperature expected by daybreak.

Radio goes to static.

Marcel Marcel, for one, welcomes the heat because the cars will die sooner. Marcel waits with arms spread wide as the widest sea, for all Marcel's children to run back to mama.

Jaye Uh-huh. Prostitution thrives in hard times.

Tilly (*to* **Natty**) I'm afraid. Really.

Natty What do you fear?

Tilly Everything. I'm afraid of cars. Motorboats. Voting.

Marcel (*to* **Jaye**) Why don't you go live in BROOKLYN with the rest of your sisters? Why don't you leave Marcel to Marcel's business?

Jaye Looks to me like Marcel hasn't had any business in a long time. Tilly. Look. He's got cobwebs sprouting from his underarms. Lack of use.

Tilly Mostly, though, I'm afraid I'll lose Jaye. And then I would just crumple up and blow away. Like a picnic napkin. We insult each other a lot, but we like it that way.

Marcel (*to* **Jaye**) I AM NOT A HE. I AM . . . MARCEL.

Natty How would you lose her? Why? Well. I guess I'm the last one to be asking those questions.

Tilly I could lose her the way I met her. In an instant.

Marcel *takes a beer from the shopping cart.*

Marcel Marcel requires retribution for your insult.

Tilly I mean, isn't that always true? One minute you know somebody, the next minute you don't. One day you're in love, the next day you're not. You look a girl in the eye and you make a snap judgement. Love makes spontaneous decisions.

Natty And so does hate. Cowardice.

Marcel Oh my little ones. Welcome to Marcel's PHILOSOPHY CORNER. Let's see. We've got one horrifically skinny almost naked queer boy and . . . oh my . . . one DRUNKEN DYKE . . . waxing poetic on the nature of our hasty, hasty hearts.

Jaye Have you got something better to say?

Tilly I met Jaye at Kennedy Airport. She was to meet a cousin from Los Angeles. I flew into New York looking for a home. I was especially unattractive that day. As I approached the ground transportation exit, I felt a hand grab my arm. I whirled around and it was Jaye. She said –

Jaye You're ugly, but you must be the one.

Tilly I couldn't tell if this was a compliment. She took my bags to her car, muttered something about an Uncle Roger.

Jaye I passed on regards from Aunt Ida.

Tilly I wondered where we were headed. She said –

Jaye The barbecue's at three.

Tilly I mean, who could argue? I began to hallucinate. Maybe I was destined to be in the back seat of a stranger's Honda Civic with no idea of where I was being taken. All I could think about was her eyes. Her funny hat. The way she gripped the steering wheel.

Jaye I stopped three times so she could vomit.

Tilly Jesus, was I *sick*. But I couldn't help it. This was completely unlike me, to be in a car with a sexy woman who was wearing a funny hat. A hat with a musical *flower* attached to its brim. Wow. And then, as I was about to pass out from the thrill of it all, she said –

Jaye I wish I'd known I had such a wacko cousin.

Tilly I blurted out, but, hey, I'm not your cousin. Stop the car. There's been a mistake.

Jaye I stopped the car.

Tilly But there was no mistake. She turned to me. I was a mess. Drool dangling from the corners of my mouth. Acne grew spontaneously, like spores. She said –

Jaye I know you're not my cousin. I was just testing the quality of your imagination.

Tilly Oh, sure, I said. But I don't even *know* you.

Jaye And why the fuck *don't* you know me? Said I.

Tilly Well. So. Why not? It was true. She looked at me and there was a conspiracy of understanding.

Jaye Don't believe her. She was squinting a lot. And she adores conspiracy theories.

Tilly And every year on that day we go back to Kennedy. Sit in tacky bars and make passes at the flight attendants.

Jaye I *love* flight attendants.

Natty *begins to douse himself with cologne.*

Marcel Oh nononono. Marcel says: please do not open Doctor Caligari's cabinet again.

Jaye Why don't you ZIP IT and DRINK UP, Marcel. Or you'll miss the bus to HELL when it rounds the corner.

Tilly Excuse me. Natty. That's your name, isn't it?

Natty Jimmy liked airports. We meant to build our vacations around cities that had remarkable airports. But we never managed to get out of New York. There was always something to be done. Always something to do right under your own nose.

Tilly Look, I didn't mean to make you feel bad. Jaye and me, we're really very fucked up. So don't use us as an example.

Natty As an example of what?

Tilly Well. You know. Whatever people use . . . other people . . . as examples of.

Jaye Natty. Listen. You really shouldn't mix colognes like that. It'll have a bad effect.

Natty Cologne sustains me. Rivers of cologne. I can't stand my own smell anymore. I want to go to meetings. I want to learn how to *like* drugs. I want to visit all the places I've had people mail me postcards from. I want to PARTICIPATE. I WANT HIM BACK.

Natty *clears the vanity with one swipe of a fist. Bottles shatter on the street.*

Marcel Marcel says: boys will be boys.

Natty My skin is . . . bubbling. The heat. THE HEAT. LOOK. I'M DEVELOPING BOILS.

Jaye *touches* **Natty** *and jumps back.*

Jaye (*really much more interested in her hand than in* **Natty**) Ouch. Christ. Tilly. We need a towel. And some cold water. This boy's . . . really hot.

Natty (*to* **Jaye**) I'm gonna burn in hell.

Jaye (*totally uninterested*) Listen. We're gonna, you know, get some help.

Natty My limbs are gonna drop off.

Tilly It's our fault. I knew it. We let that night happen and in doing so, allowed the weather to take over.

Marcel And why the fuck *shouldn't* the weather take over? I've already seen a ghost tonight. Nothing can compare.

Natty *grabs* **Jaye**.

Natty You saw it, didn't you.

Jaye Yes.

Natty You watched him die.

Jaye (*she pulls away*) Not . . . exactly.

Tilly Yes. We did watch him die. The sky split open. The temperature rose. And nothing's been the same since.

Jaye Well. *That's* true enough. Lately, our lovemaking has come to resemble something out of Genet.

Marcel Mama said there'd be days like this. There'd be days like this, Marcel's mama said.

Natty What was it like? Tell me.

Jaye We called the police. That's what it was like.

Natty No. I mean. What was it like? To see him die. I didn't. See it. I should have.

Tilly Don't do this. It's not necessary.

Natty It is necessary. I've learned practically nothing, it's true. But I do know that. Tell me something. Anything.

Tilly We watched from above. We thought we were safe.

Jaye I drank beer and thought . . . how lucky I am not to be him.

Tilly We called the police. We did. But by that time, there was nothing left to protect us from.

Natty How could you. How could you . . . *watch?*

Jaye How could you run?

Tilly And you know, tell me something. What would you have done? If you were us, if you were a couple of girls holed up in a crappy apartment? Huh?

Natty I . . . I would have . . . run. Again. And again. I have no pride.

Natty *cries. A silence, as* **Tilly** *and* **Marcel** *busy themselves with anything but* **Natty**. **Jaye**, *forced to take action, pats* **Natty** *half-heartedly on his back.*

Jaye We saw you a lot, you and your lover. You shopped at all the food stores we couldn't afford. We envied your clothing. We fantasised about what art you'd collect. And each time we saw you we said, we really must invite them up for a drink.

Natty I was 30 before I told anybody except Jimmy that I was gay. Nobody knew.

Jaye That's what we all think. Nobody knows. We wear it like it's a medal of honour. We're sick to do it, but we do it anyway. And then one day, we get well. Shake the shame right outta our hair and wonder, well, why in the fuck did we ever let it get the best of us? The trick is to get rid of it. *Before* the point of implosion. Before it eats us to pieces.

Natty I'm in so many pieces I don't remember what it's like to be whole.

Tilly And so we said, we really must invite them up for a drink. But we didn't. What did we think would happen?

Headlights beam directly at **Marcel.**

Marcel And once again, Marcel lifts Marcel's weary shell of a body and entertains the troops. Marcel wears a dress so Marcel can gather all of humankind underneath it. Oh my lonesome dove, are *you* going to help Marcel pass time? Let me tell you honey, this absolute COW of a dyke called Marcel an anachronism. What do you think of THAT? Well. At least I am recognisable. AT LEAST I AM THE LAST OF THE MOHICANS. I saw it, too. DO THEY THINK I DIDN'T SEE IT? That night, Marcel was collecting business like it was stardust. Marcel was BUSY. And Marcel saw the blade strike its target and Marcel hit the street so fast Marcel didn't notice that Marcel was lying in TRASH. Animal innards. Guts. COW BLOOD. Marcel sank in entrails for the better part of an hour before the cops came to drag Marcel off. Marcel sat in a precinct. Marcel sat in a straight-back chair whilst no gentlemanly police officer gave Marcel as much as a HANDY WIPE. Marcel stank. Marcel was humiliated and covered in debris. But still. Still. Marcel saw everything and in the end, all

Marcel saw was that cool steel blade. And Marcel realised. MARCEL KNEW THAT . . . I . . . knew that. I was wearing a dress and some bad falsies and every ounce of self-preservation kicked in and and and . . . there was me and my dress and . . . I could cut myself no slack. I sank. I went way way down that night. DON'T THEY THINK I KNOW THAT? Oh. My speedy traveller. Shut off your engine and ignite my transmission. Teach me to DRIVE. Take it all away. Take me HOME.

A sudden explosion of blinding hot white light. Just for an instant, and then it is gone. Radio static is heard.

Radio . . . 167 degrees and rising. Unconfirmed reports from Hoboken, Piscataway and Edison, New Jersey of automobiles spontaneously combusting. And this just in . . . at Kennedy Airport, a Delta seven-forty-seven exploded on takeoff. At Port Authority, a Greyhound bus bound for Lincoln, Nebraska melted within seconds of entering the Holland Tunnel. Current Central Park temperature 167 and RISING.

Radio goes to static. A brief silence. Lights down on all but **Marcel**.

Marcel Marcel Hughes. H-U-G-H-E-S. Yes. That is my . . . actual . . . name. I was born at 227–27 Horace Harding Expressway in Queens, New York. My mother, Sally Hughes, was a practical nurse. Or practically a nurse. I can never remember which. My father, whose name I cannot bring myself to utter, was a small businessman. Very small. He owned a shed, took it to a corner, and called it a news-stand.

Lights up on **Jaye**.

Jaye My lover and I were watching television. Yeah. That's right. She's my lover. You got a problem with that? Okay. So we're watching television and we hear this noise from the street. I hear somebody say: FAGGOT. I always hear that word when it's said. Always.

Lights up on **Tilly**.

Tilly Jaye and I were watching television. Well, Jaye was watching. I was looking out the windows, as usual. Excuse me? No. I do not SPY on people in the street. Well. Actually, I do. But. Anyway. Jaye was watching a basketball game and cursing herself because, you know, it was such a dykey thing to be watching.

Marcel It was very dark. And I was observing this from quite some distance. Pardon moi? Oh. I was . . . walking. I was taking a walk. I often take walks in the neighbourhood. What? Yes. I LIKE to walk. So. I can tell you that he was definitely Hispanic. Or a light-skinned black. Pretty skin. Smooth. Gorgeous. A big guy. Don't you just LOVE big men?

Jaye I saw this guy stabbing this other guy. The guy with the knife was a fair-haired tall white guy. Maybe six foot three. Broad shoulders. Strawberry blond with freckles. Good looking. Like the kind of jerk I used to date before I got wise. I remember thinking I hadn't seen hair that colour for a long time.

Tilly He must have been, oh I don't know, 19 or 20. Small. Delicate. Wiry. With devastating hands. I adore hands. And this kid had glorious hands. And he worked out. Great body. Little rippling muscles all over him. But those hands. Hmmm. Wondrous.

Marcel Oh yeah. He was a FAT motherfucker. And old. That sucker was OLD. 45, at least. But I think jolly old fat men are sexy.

Jaye Other than that, he was pretty nondescript. *You* know the type. Played some college football. Has a beer gut, but otherwise, you know, he's in pretty decent shape. He was attractive, and I couldn't understand how somebody who was kind of attractive could do such a shitty thing.

Tilly I can't tell you much about his face, but if you showed me his hands I'd know. You see somebody use his hands to kill and you don't forget it.

Lights up on **Natty**.

Natty Do you know what I recall most vividly? That Jimmy called me an asshole. Those were his final words to me, I think. I think . . . why did we survive AIDS, Jimmy and me, to come to *this?* There's no dignity left. I'd like to go home now if I may. I can't tell you what he looked like. I barely saw him. I've got a lot to bury.

Boy *enters. He stands before the group first in profile, then full face. Then he holds out his hands to them. The group, in unison, with the exception of* **Natty**, *point fingers at* **Boy**. **Natty** *bows his head, unable to look.*

All except Natty That's him.

Lights down on all but **Boy**.

Boy Makes no difference to me *who* I kill. I could tell you that it was a *personal* thing. I could tell you about how goddamned pretty the blade is at night. Out in the open air. But I'm not *going* to talk about *those* things. I'm gonna let you put me on the news and I'm gonna nod my head at a lot of stupid people talking about misunderstanding and compassion and bad upbringings and I'm gonna fucking laugh out loud. What? Who said something about bias crimes? What the fuck is BIAS? This is about HATE. And there isn't a lawyer or a doctor or any fucked up fucking do-gooder alive who can do a damned thing about it. You wanna fight me, you got to FIGHT me. Lock me up. Come on. Do it. You can take away my blade, but I'm still out there. There's more of me back where I come from.

Lights down on **Boy**. *Lights up on the rest of the scene.*

Empty beer bottles and cans scattered everywhere. **Natty** *has taken to cutting* **Marcel***'s pantyhose into tiny pieces.* **Marcel** *sits in the shopping cart. He drinks beer.* **Jaye** *spins him around in circles.* **Tilly** *sits among the remnants of the broken cologne bottles. She takes shards of glass and dabs them to her wrists, her neck, any pulse point she can find.*

Tilly I've never smelled a Chanel perfume before. Hmmmm. It's not as . . . old smelling . . . as I imagined.

Natty That's number 19. An elusive scent. Not everyone can wear it.

Tilly Yeah, well. It suits the street. (*Dabs a shard of glass against her wrist.*) Shit. It cut me.

Marcel Oooooweeeee. Marcel is a dizzy miss lizzie. Stop the world honey, 'cause Marcel wants to get OFF.

Jaye We're creating a breeze, Marcel. If we spin long and hard enough, we'll make a typhoon that will carry us to . . . who knows where.

Marcel Take me to the river.

Jaye (*stopping the cart*) River's dried up. We could *walk* across to Jersey.

Tilly Jaye. The Chanel CUT me. I dabbed it on and it fucking CUT me.

Marcel Don't you bother about that my little Sapphist. Chanel is not an equal opportunity parfumière. Chanel knows which wrists it belongs on.

Tilly Oh God WHY did we choose to live in a neighbourhood full of gay men?

Jaye Because we think we *are* gay men.

Tilly Don't start in on me again, Jaye. We're snobs. That's why. We don't even have enough money to buy brand-name toilet paper and we think it's more refined to live with faggots. I swear. I feel like Eliza Doolittle in drag. AND THERE'S NO MORE BEER. WE DRANK 27 CASES AND WE'RE NOT DRUNK.

Jaye Look. There are no lights on in Jersey.

Radio static, very loud. Then:

Radio . . . supports have collapsed. Repeat: the George Washington, Triborough, Brooklyn, Manhattan, Williamsburgh and Queensboro bridges have collapsed. Current Central Park temperature 180 degrees. Repeat 180 and rising.

Marcel Good. So much for the bridge and tunnel crowd.

Natty The neighbourhood is ours again. You'd think I'd be happy about that. But I'm not.

Tilly I'm bleeding. It doesn't hurt, though. You always think you have time. You know, to do certain things. Say whatever needs to be said.

Jaye You do say whatever needs to be said. You talk in your sleep.

Tilly What do I say?

Jaye You talk about . . . Melanie Griffith. Flight attendants. Tarts.

Tilly I've barely gotten used to the way you sleep. And now it's gotten so hot we *can't* sleep. Shit. I can never adjust to change.

Natty *collapses.*

Marcel Girls. GIRLS. EMERGENCY.

Marcel *tries to push himself towards* **Natty**, *who sits bolt upright and speaks with great urgency.*

Natty Things I ought to have done but didn't: buy a Jaguar adopt a puppy become an Episcopalian take communion and I should have been promiscuous when promiscuity was good should have called my dad before he croaked should have gone to law school should have loved him truer cleaner braver should have. Could have. Didn't. BE HANDSOMER LOSE WEIGHT SPEAK MY MIND FIGHT FIGHT FIGHT BACK.

Marcel Marcel says: GET ME OUT OF THIS FUCKING CART.

Tilly *helps* **Marcel** *out of the shopping cart.* **Jaye** *touches* **Natty**, *tentatively, as if she's touching a bug.*

Jaye *He's* awfully hot.

Natty This is the way it happens. With strangers. One minute you know somebody. The next minute you're dead.

Sudden explosion of hot white light. Silence. **Marcel** *and* **Tilly** *hold each other. Headlights beam directly at* **Marcel**.

Marcel That's the biggest motherfucking car I've ever seen.

Tilly It's shimmering.

Marcel Oh my deep-pocketed traveller. Tell Marcel you are the richest man in the UNIVERSE. Oh my road warrior, the world is burning up and Marcel doesn't want to miss the FIRE.

Tilly It's glowing. Jaye. That car is GLOWING.

Marcel GLOW MY WAY OH DANNY BOY. BURN WITH ME.

A car horn is heard. Silence. The horn sounds again.

Tilly They're honking for you.

Marcel I'm not going.

Tilly Why not?

Marcel I played Mystery Date in high school. I know the bum's waiting for me behind the door. I KNOW IT.

Natty (*to* **Jaye**) Tell me why I ran away. Tell me why I'm still running.

Jaye There's no end to it. Never has been.

Natty I'm feverish.

Jaye Uh-huh.

Natty I like that. Feels like something's . . . happening.

Tilly Look Marcel. You've got a fucking CUSTOMER. When's the last time one of those rolled through?

Marcel Marcel is very particular.

Tilly Who do you think's gonna drive by? There aren't exactly limitless options at this point.

Marcel I didn't think I'd live to see the day when a lesbian became my pimp.

Tilly Times change.

Car horn sounds.

Natty Is there . . . something happening?

Jaye The city's falling apart. Nothing new there.

Natty Something's ending. Something's busting up.

Jaye Yeah. I feel that way every time I take the subway.

Car horn sounds.

Marcel (*considering this carefully*) I like to travel. I like to FLY.

Tilly Wow. That car is . . . LEVITATING.

Marcel Oh mymymy. WAIT FOR ME, PETER PAN. Marcel's going to places where there is no slime to sink down into. Where the big girl's shop is always OPEN.

Marcel *tidies himself up, starts towards the headlights. An explosion of hot white light, and he's gone.*

Radio . . . no longer registering. Temperatures can no longer be measured. 200 degrees at last reading. Last reading. Last reading. Barometric pressure is at a standstill. Jones Beach has fallen into the Atlantic. We advise all residents to –

Radio goes to static.

Tilly *gathers up a pair of* **Marcel's** *pantyhose and wraps them around her wrist.*

Tilly I can't stop bleeding.

Natty This is the way it happens. This way.

Tilly But it's slow.

Natty With strangers.

Tilly And unpredictable. Shit. Now what. I'm turning into a SHRINE. I'll bleed forever and people will kneel at my feet. They'll light candles. Make offerings.

Natty I'm shivering. Sick. I'm paying for something.

Jaye Bullshit. We never pay for anything. Be quiet.

Tilly *kneels at the ceramic basin. She submerges her head in it. While* **Natty** *speaks, she bangs her head into the basin. Slowly. Rhythmically.*

Natty (*a great realisation*) Something's busting up. I'm . . . imploding. A fluorescent bulb I am a bulb a light a sickness an arrested development an ember the world in my pocket and and and I WANT HIM BACK I WANT A CHANCE TO NOT DIE IN THIS HEAT I WANT I WANT –

Jaye Shut up. SHUT UP. MY GIRLFRIEND'S GOT FUCKING STIGMATA. Shut. The fuck. Up.

Music in: Intro: Prelude to Love/Could This Be Magic (*Donna Summer*). **Tilly** *snaps to attention. Her hair and face are soaked with water and bits of blood.* **Tilly** *and* **Natty** *bop along to the music. It fills them with an odd sense of determination and direction.*

Jaye What the fuck . . .

Tilly I'm melting. I'm bleeding and wet and God. I LOVE THIS SONG.

Natty Dress me.

Jaye It's too hot for clothes. Be quiet. Tilly. TILLY. LOOK AT ME.

Tilly I can't. I'm too busy falling apart.

Jaye Why won't you look at me?

Tilly Don't know. Don't know.

Natty Clothe me. In white.

Jaye And where is this music coming from? WHERE?

Tilly Nineteen seventy-something. Before we were mean.

Natty Before we lost time. Please. Dress me up and take me to a DISCO.

Natty *and* **Tilly** *continue to dance.* **Tilly** *removes her blouse.*

Jaye What are you doing?

Tilly Melting. Moulting. Something.

Tilly *undresses completely. She rifles through the clothing rack. She finds a dazzling white suit.* **Natty** *begins to shake violently. He falls to his knees.* **Jaye** *cradles him.*

Jaye I've never held a man in my arms like this. Never wanted to. Still not sure I want to.

Natty So cold. So . . . fucking . . . cold. We're burning up.

Jaye Have I always been this mean? Have I? God. If it's true I'll slit my throat.

Tilly *puts on the man's suit jacket. The pants. They are ridiculously large on her. She goes to* **Jaye** *and* **Natty**, *kneels beside them. Her hair, if possible, seems to get wetter.*

Jaye (*touching* **Tilly**'*s face*) Baby. You look . . . deranged. You're so wet.

Tilly Hey. You never touch me in public.

Jaye Things change.

Natty *continues to shiver, but he's happy, he's smiling. The music is loud and glorious.* **Jaye** *kisses* **Tilly**.

Tilly Wow. You kissed me. And I'm not even drunk.

Natty Take me to a disco and play this song over and over. Make it sweet. Make it pretty. Make it count. Help me. Clothe me. CLOTHE ME.

Tilly *and* **Jaye** *dress* **Natty** *in* **Tilly**'*s clothing. Her blouse. Her slacks. Whatever. Strangely, they fit him rather well.*

Tilly Water and blood pouring out of me. I feel so clean. I'm shedding myself.

Jaye You're glorious. A mess, but glorious.

Natty My heart is breaking it's busting up I'm fine I'm happy I need . . . contact . . . make contact. MAKE CONTACT. PLEASE. PLEASE. MAKE THEM UNDERSTAND. WE ARE NOT . . . WE ARE NOT COWARDS.

Jaye *removes* **Tilly**'*s jacket. She then removes her own blouse.*

Natty I can't stand all this. Beauty. I can't.

Jaye *grasps* **Natty**'*s hand, tight. She bends to take* **Tilly**'*s breast into her mouth.*

Tilly Oh God. We're so close to the edge, we can't even see it coming.

Jaye *and* **Tilly** *begin to make love. The music continues, insistent.* **Natty** *holds on to* **Jaye**'*s hand.* **Jimmy** *enters. He's dressed in white from head to toe. He holds a knife.*

Natty Jimmy. Oh Jimmy where have you gone. Where are you going to.

Jimmy I'm on my way. Be on my way with me.

Jimmy *pulls* **Natty** *to his feet.* **Jaye** *and* **Tilly** *continue to make love.*

Natty Where are we going?

Jimmy We're going to 10 West. We have a date.

Natty But I lost my hair. I can't go anywhere.

Jimmy We're going to make you well. Take this.

Jimmy *gives* **Natty** *the knife.*

Natty Jimmy. This is a knife. A weapon.

Jimmy It's a beginning. Tear up the world for me. Make your mark.

Jimmy *leads* **Natty** *to the enormous map of the meat packing district. He takes* **Natty**'*s hand, lightly tracing over the map with the knife.*

Jimmy It's easy to get someplace if you know where you're going. Look. Look how we're gliding through.

Natty *slashes through the map with the knife. Again. And again.*

Jimmy Time to fly, Natty Weldon.

Natty Lift me.

Jimmy *lifts* **Natty** *into his arms. They step through the map. They're gone.* **Jaye** *and* **Tilly** *are a splendid sight amid the ruin. A glorious flash of white light and they disappear.*

The torn up map begins to shake, violently.

Blackout. End of play.

Weldon Rising

Although *Weldon Rising* was written in and about New York City, I think of it now as my first London play. It came about as a result of a two-week trip to the Royal Court Theatre in November 1991, at which time I attended a rehearsed reading of my play *Awake*. Apart from the instructive time I spent working on that play at the Court, something else happened over the course of those two weeks. I fell in love. Subsequently, returning to New York and going about the business of *living* there was never again quite the same.

I began to see New York, despite all the excitement it still held for me, as a city whose time was very nearly up. It was a place that had, perhaps, stood still too long in its increasingly hostile tracks. When the mounting urban paranoia that had paralysed other sections of the city predictably, and sadly, charged into the hitherto gay-sympathetic enclave of the far West Village, I decided I'd had enough. If Greenwich Village wasn't safe for us, nowhere was safe. My growing frustration over how we might best conduct our lives, and still manage to love in the midst of violence and its inevitable by-product, fear, led me to finally write *Weldon Rising*.

The text raises several controversial questions about the nature of fear and its connection to violence, and those questions, in turn, led to some startling discoveries early in the production process. Auditions revealed the extent to which stereotypical characterisations of gays and lesbians still pervade our consciousness. The director of *Weldon Rising*, Penny Ciniewicz, and I saw a good many actors, some of whom were openly gay, for the role of Natty. To our surprise, most of these actors either camped-up the part outrageously or chose to portray Natty as a snivelling, shrinking nonentity. It did not occur to any of them that it is possible to fight cowardice through *action*, rather than through self-pitying reflection. Similarly, most of the women who were seen for the roles of Jaye and Tilly chose to portray essentially stereotypical butch/femme types. Penny and I began to find this unfortunately predictable, as we came to understand just how deeply rooted is the fear of complex, politically ambivalent gay characters who simply *are* gay.

It is much easier for audiences – both straight *and* gay – to accept lesbian and gay characters who obsess and fret about their gayness as an *issue* (and who, as a result, enable an audience to feel they are on solid ground) than it is to accept lesbians and gay characters who sometimes 'misbehave' and who do not present themselves as sexless, vaguely martyred but politically hip individuals who manipulate empathy and equate it with victimhood. That kind of characterisation creates a false empathy in good liberal audiences, and that empathy is built on guilt. *Weldon Rising* is not a politically correct gay issue play, nor does it trade on collective guilt, which is why I suspect it was either completely ignored or poorly received by the London gay press. That the mainstream critical and public response to the play was overwhelmingly favourable undoubtedly intensified the negative response of a small section of the gay community. But *that* is another debate for another day.

In discussions with audiences both in Liverpool and London, recurring questions about *Weldon Rising* began to emerge, such as: does Natty commit suicide at the end of the play? Or its variation: does Natty go to heaven or to hell? These questions intrigued me rather than annoyed me, and, like the choice various actors made to queen-up the text, they became a kind of subliminal audience litmus test. Of course, I find it impossible to imagine that Natty commits *suicide*, as the very thought of it defies the play's logic throughout. Quite simply, Natty, having finally gathered the courage to *make* the decision to leave, summons Jimmy, and they go elsewhere. Where? Literally, Natty slashes his way through the world, and whether or not he and Jimmy make their way to heaven is irrelevant. They move on, and though it must clearly be to a better place, it is not necessarily to a *divine* place.

Similarly, I could not begin to understand the notion that some people saw the character of Boy as a closet homosexual. There is nothing in the text to indicate this at all. Because he appears to flirt with Jimmy, does that make him gay? Absolutely not. Killers employ various methods of flirtation, sexual or otherwise, with their victims, which is the trait that enables them to perpetrate violent acts so effectively in the first place. If the Boy is able to disarm Jimmy with charm, he has relaxed his guard. It's a simple equation. The Boy, at least intially, is curious about the gay men, in the way that we are curious and a bit repelled by things that scare us or are unfamiliar to us. And I believe that the Boy does not intend to commit murder until the very moment he does it.

Another recurring question was: why is Jaye so unsympathetic and Tilly so crazy? I find Jaye to be among the most sympathetic characters in the play, merely because she *behaves* rather than postures. Is it unsympathetic to reveal your distaste for certain people and attitudes? I think not. Actually, as we discovered in rehearsals, the more Jaye *plays* at sympathy or attempts to justify her behaviour, the more unpleasant she is. Similarly, it is very easy to make the assumption that Tilly is a neurotic mess rather than a naturally *curious* person who says exactly what she thinks at all times. Is she *crazy* because she chooses to sit at her window and drink beer for a couple of weeks? Again, I think not. She, like the others, is extremely moral, and her curiosity about the truth of every matter (or its denial) is what fuels her, not an unreasonable neurosis about the size of Marcel's pantyhose. As a result, our rehearsals bore out a general playing rule for the text: the more matter-of-fact and without judgement the presentation, the less bizarre the entire scenario becomes. But this is difficult to achieve in a theatrical climate where so much of what is written depends on an actor's ability to create an hermetically sealed and *judgmental* take on a character. What *Weldon Rising* asks of its actors is to give over traditional notions of individual character *development* to the greater good of the *arc* of the play. It requires a suspension of *comment* on the text and moreover, demands an attention to ensemble playing, especially towards the end, that takes a group of very brave actors to achieve.

With this in mind, my heartfelt thanks go to the original cast of *Weldon Rising*, all of whom took a great leap of faith even when, from time to time, they struggled with the material. My debt of gratitude to Penny Ciniewicz, who directed the rehearsed reading of the play and then took on its production, is immense. My thanks as well to the many people, both at the Royal Court and the Liverpool Playhouse, who made the production possible, including: Carl Miller, Stephen Jeffreys, Ramin Gray, Kate Rowland, Elyse Dodgson, Max Stafford-Clark, Gemma Bodinetz and Stephen Daldry. And finally, my love and thanks to Mel Kenyon, without whom the play would not exist.

Phyllis Nagy was born in New York City and now lives in London. Recent work includes *Weldon Rising* (Royal Court Theatre; Liverpool Playhouse); *Entering Queens* (Gay Sweatshop, London and UK tour); and the Mobil award-winning *Disappeared*. She is currently writing *The Strip* for the Royal Court and for Radio 4; *Never Land* for Hampstead Theatre; and a teleplay, *Bait and Switch*, for BBC 2. In America, she recently adapted Nathaniel Hawthorne's *The Scarlet Letter* for the Denver Centre Theatre, and has written *Trip's Cinch* for the Actor's Theatre of Louisville. Her latest play, *Butterfly Kiss*, will be produced at the Almeida Theatre, London, in 1994. Phyllis is a member playwright of New Dramatists, New York.

Lightning Source UK Ltd.
Milton Keynes UK
11 July 2010

156822UK00001B/87/P